# NORTHAMPTON GOLF CLUB

## THE COMPETITIVE GOLF SCENE AT KETTERING ROAD AND HARLESTONE 1969-2001

by MARTIN JOHN IZZARD

A PERSONAL COLLECTION OF EMOTIONS
AND EVENTS CONTRIBUTING TO MY LIFE
AND A GREAT GOLF CLUB.

# ACKNOWLEDGEMENTS

I would like to thank the following for their emotional and physical contribution throughout the last thirty years. This book would not have been possible without their often timely, at times invisible and thoughtful help: Bobby Bason, Jack Bird for chapter thirty, Andy Carter, Jeannie Craddock for compelation of recent scores, David Dare, Bob Glass for the photographs of the Kettering Road course, Mike Gallagher, James Hallwood for proof reading, Martin Harris, Roger Hart for the 1996 Hollingsworth photographs, Rose Heath for chapter thirty one, Derek Holland, Jon Lloyd for proof reading, Glenn Keates, Tom Knight, Alan Linney, Alf Lovelady, the late Audrey Jean Izzard, Liz Izzard, Sean Malherbe for administrative assistance, Ian Popple for the Onion Spinney photograph, Gil Sibley, Jeremy Shepherd, Gary Slinn for the photo of Harlestone house, Tony Stevens, the late Jane Anne Izzard, Bob Willoughby, and many other supporters and friends too numerous to mention.

With a book of this size and complexity there will inevitably be some minor errors, hopefully these will not detract from the aim of the book to provide a good factual and emotional read. The publication of this book would not have been possible without the support of many advertisers and subscribers; your contribution is greatly appreciated by all of the local golf community.

# DEDICATIONS

THIS BOOK IS DEDICATED TO ALL GOLFERS

FROM NORTHAMPTONSHIRE OUR COUNTY

OF SPIRES AND SQUIRES, WHO HAVE IN THE

PAST, TO THOSE PRESENT AND TO THOSE IN

THE FUTURE WHO DEMONSTRATE THE

TRUE VALUES AND TRADITIONS OF THIS

GREAT GAME.


MARTIN JOHN IZZARD

MARCH 2002

Published by the Northampton Golf Club
2002
All righes Reserved
ISBN 0-9520291-1-1

Printed and Bound in Great Britain by
Woolnough Bookbinding Limited
Express Works, Church Street, Irthlingborough, Northants NN9 5SE

# CONTENTS

# INTRODUCTION

This book describes the last thirty years of the twentieth century golfing at Northampton G.C. It also documents the trophy winners throughout the history of the club, the friends and events that I have had the good fortune to become involved with. It may hopefully be perceived in due course as an addition to the excellent History of The Northampton Golf Club, so beautifully and lovingly prepared by Gil Sibley, a great stalwart of the Club. The results sections for the competitions have deliberately left with spaces for those members who like to keep a record of those fortunate trophy winners.

As I have put this book together over the last three winters, I have been amazed at how the nature of the golf game has changed. The Club's record books have been a vast knowledge base to draw from and you can feel the passion of the various workers in many of the beautifully hand written records and the recent computer records dating back over one hundred years. The rules of play, the equipment and golf swings have changed considerably, together with a greater number of entries to competitions. For instance sheltering was permitted for several decades and in the sixties the Northampton Cup final was often played for by only a handful of players. Quite a different scenario to our current problems of slow play and having to queue up for a starting time in the monthly medal!

The chapters on the individual competitions are set out in the time-honored sequence as presented at the annual trophies night. The winners names have been taken from the Club's trophy boards and the winning scores extracted from the Clubs record books and information available. Sadly the scores between 1946-1953 and 1990-2001 have "disappeared". These are followed by the many other events/characters and golf happenings which have occurred over the last thirty golfing years. During this time we have experienced the move from our old wooden clubhouse and "hills and holes course" at Kettering Road to our marvellous new clubhouse and course at Harlestone. This book attempts to capture the golf scene, the feelings and fun encountered at both sites. Many members have delved deep in to their memories to assist the author; I thank you all most sincerely.

As the Club moves forward in this new century, let us ensure that we keep the balance of tradition linked to future developments in one of Northamptonshire's great Clubs, where the many different elements of golf are catered for.

*Trophy Winners 2001 with Captain Geoff Keates (centre left) and President Tom Knight (centre right)*

# CHAPTER 1

# SPRING SCRATCH CUP / CLUB CHAMPIONSHIP

"Be the ball, see your destiny" The Film Caddyshack

**F.BOSTOCK and A.E.Phipps originally presented this trophy as the Coronation Challenge Bowl in 1901 for the best scratch score over eighteen holes played on the Saturday or Sunday in the spring meeting. The trophy was renamed as the Club Championship in 1974 and has become the Blue Ribbon/Premier Trophy to win at the Club for low handicap players. The trophy is now awarded for the best score over 36 holes of medal play.**

During the early 70's the trophy this trophy was won by the likes of Norman Jones, Walter Clarke, Roy Miles and Alan Parker. Walter Clarke was a tremendous supporter of golf at the club and played of a handicap of 1 in his prime. Walter was always encouraging to young players and encouraged them to push themselves to the maximum of their abilities and to take an interest in many diverse areas other than golf. As far as my young memory goes Roy Miles was a relaxed and gentleman man who always had time for his friends and played the game in a relaxed and friendly manner. Now for A.J.Parker who was known to his golfing compatriots, most notably the late Dick Biggin, as Powka! Alan was and still is a player who has never lost the desire to win. This has been exemplified by the number of Powka entries on the trophy boards at the club; we have recently not felt his presence too often at the club.

Jim Pettigrew was a fine player and has always supported golf in Northamptonshire. He along with Richard Halliday, Richard Aitken was a winning member of the Anglian League 1st Team who won the Daily Telegraph Salver in 1972.

Kevin Newman burst on the scene in 1978 as he became a County first team player and helped to encourage the author to better golfing practices.

This resulted in the last victory for the County B Team in 1980 where Kevin and the author made a major contribution (see chapter twenty eight). Kevin in fact won this trophy twice. However, the affliction of the dreaded shank has occasionally affected his abilities recently.

A mixture of young guns such as Mark Britten, Gary Addington and the older guard of Alan Linney, Bob Killip, dominated the 1980s. The talented Scottish doctor Lance Sloan put in a brief appearance in 1984 and probably would have won the title on more occasions if he had not moved away from the area. Lance in fact nearly broke the course record on the old course twice. The well-known difficulties of the 197 yard seventeenth and 455 yard eighteenth holes cost him bogeys on both occasions, however.

The last decade of the twentieth century was essentially dominated by the youngsters who found the new course at Harlestone very much to their liking as Glenn Keates, Simon Tootell and Jon Lloyd developed from their Junior days in to quality players. Glenn became only the fourth player in the history of the competition to complete a hat trick of victories together with P.D.Riddall, F.C.Roe and J.W.Taylor and the first player to complete the feat as the Club Championship. During this decade Dominic Jessup and myself represented the old guard. I was fortunate to become the only player to have won the trophy on both golf courses. I would not have won the trophy in 1991 if my tee shot on the twelfth had not bounced back in bounds having pitched on top of the wall adjoining the farmers field.

Dominic actually completed the much-wanted double of this trophy and the Match Play championship in this his only Club Championship victory in 1993.

There have been three eighteen hole play-offs for the title where Alan Linney, Andy (NR) Carter and Andy Limbert were triumphal in what were all one sided events. The play off in 1985 was a grudge match following an altercation outside the clubhouse between Alan Linney and David Dare. The play off attracted a large gallery, which appeared to represent the views of "both sides". The event was effectively over when David succumbed to a quintuple bogey nine on the par four second hole having become stuck in a bush. The Chronicle and Echo paper cruelly running the headlines on the top of the back page "He who Dare's Loses Twice". The details behind this story are given in chapter 2.

A similar golfing scenario affected Andy Carter's chances in 1998 when he was unable to escape from the deep rough on the right of the par five third hole. His chance of victory had gone when he finished the hole with a treble bogey eight. Andy was however more successful in 1989 where a solid round of golf watched by a large contingent from the Carter family on Ryder Cup Saturday produced his one and only victory.

The Millennium winner was Glenn Keates who retained the title the following year in fine style, with a total of 139 five under par, on a wet and changeable day. The morning rounds of 70 gross were the keys to both victories; the 2001 morning round was a great score in bad conditions.

*Club Champions 1989, Andy Carter, Medal (right)
with Dominic Jessup, Matchplay.*

Glenn was initially leading by three shots after the morning round and eventually won by six strokes ahead of fellow County player and playing partner Simon Tootell. These good rounds reduced Glenn's handicap to plus one. The following day Glenn carried on his good form that weekend, in an Anglian League match versus Cambridgeshire where he displayed the form and behaviour we at Northampton Golf Club love to see. His father Geoff (Captain 2001) and Mother Judy (Lady Captain 1997) were very proud of their son's marvellous weekend, when he was totally committed to the Club & County. Glenn is now the six times winner of this trophy, a great feat in the last ten years from 1992-2001. I suspect a County Captain in the making.

Junior Captain Alex Izzard's "challenge" for the trophy ended on the ninth hole in the afternoon when he was struck on the back of the head by the Junior Organiser Jon Lloyd's tee shot. A visit to Accident and Emergency was required where they confirmed mild concussion and therefore no golf for a couple of days. Poor Jon felt so guilty, apart from having a story to deliver at the Junior A.G.M! The following morning, as Alex fuzzily examined the golf shaped lump on the back of his head, and stated "Cor that was some hit" I wondered whether he was referring to his head injury or friend Jon Lloyd's 290 yards tee shot? A week to the day and almost at the same time, the poor lad collapsed at the club and fell down the back stairs towards the men's locker room. He was discovered by the unfortunate Martin Harris, and rushed to hospital in an ambulance. The author and Jon Lloyd spent the next five hours at the hospital where he made a complete recovery, the brain scan confirming that he had one, which was also the normal brain of a seventeen-year-old!

It is interesting to note that the winners of the non-handicap competitions have come from players who are coming in to their prime at younger and younger ages. For example in the last thirty years over fifty per cent of the winners have come from previous Junior members. This probably reflects the improvement in standards of preparation for golf and a deeper knowledge of the mechanics of the swing. Developments in equipment design such as large headed drivers and cavity-backed clubs have also made a significant difference to the way the game is played. The discussions in the bar on the relative merits of the new equipment has promoted a challenge match between the young players with the old equipment against the old players with the new equipment, watch this space!

The striking of the ball is one element though good putting remains the key to achieving the best score. I have over the last thirty years listened to player's descriptions of games of golf where the best rounds are nearly always obtained when fewer putts are taken. This has certainly been the route to win Northampton's Club Championship.

# Spring Scratch Cup/Club Championship

| YEAR | WINNER | YEAR | WINNER |
|------|--------|------|--------|
| 1902 | H.H.O.COOKSON | 1954 | R.J.PATERSON* 160 (PO 162) |
| 1903 | N.DAWSON 89 | 1955 | B.COOKSLEY 78 |
| 1904 | D.C.SCROGGIE 79 | 1956 | D.C.SOUTHEY 78 |
| 1905 | D.C.SCROGGIE 79 | 1957 | N.JONES 75 |
| 1906 | E.N.BOSTOCK 87 | 1958 | N.JONES |
| 1907 | A.E.ANDERSON 87 | 1959 | S.PANTHER |
| 1908 | N.F.BOSTOCK | 1960 | D.C.SOUTHEY |
| 1909 | H.MOBBS 85 | 1962 | R.G.AITKEN* 74 (PO 70) |
| 1910 | E.N.BOSTOCK | 1963 | S.PANTHER 75 |
| 1911 | L.BOSTOCK 87 | 1964 | L.A.JOHNSON 77 |
| 1912 | J.S.GOULDBOURNE 91 | 1965 | R.G.AITKEN |
| 1913 | W.H.J.BUNTING 90 | 1966 | L.A.JOHNSON |
| 1914 | P.D.RIDDALL | 1967 | B.N.JONES |
|      | WORLD WAR 1 | 1968 | W.A.CLARKE |
| 1920 | P.D.RIDDALL 80 | 1969 | N.JONES |
| 1921 | P.D.RIDDALL 77 | 1970 | N.JONES |
| 1922 | T.R.TAYLOR 84 | 1971 | W.A.CLARKE |
| 1923 | P.D.RIDDALL | 1972 | J.M.PETTIGREW |
| 1924 | P.D.RIDDALL78 | 1973 | R.E.MILES |
| 1925 | G.SOUTAR 79 | 1974 | J.M.PETTIGREW 74-79 |
| 1926 | C.N.LOAKE 83 | 1975 | A.J.PARKER 76-75 |
| 1927 | H.BROOMFIELD 79 | 1976 | J.A.COSTIN 72-78 |
| 1928 | H.J.D.ARKELL 76 | 1977 | A.J.PARKER 76-78 |
| 1929 | G.N.SOMERS 81 | 1978 | K.NEWMAN 75 |
| 1930 | F.C.ROE | 1979 | M.J.IZZARD 73-79 |
| 1931 | F.C.ROE 76 | 1980 | K.NEWMAN 76-69 |
| 1932 | G.N.SOMERS 76 | 1981 | R.J.C.KILLIP 75-74 |
| 1933 | G.W.MINNEY | 1982 | M.BRITTEN 79-70 |
| 1934 | F.C.ROE | 1983 | A.J.LINNEY 74-79 |
| 1935 | F.C.ROE | 1984 | R.L.SLOAN 67-76 |
| 1936 | F.C.ROE 77 | 1985 | A.J.LINNEY 74-79* |
| 1937 | H.P.PASSMORE 72 | 1986 | G.P.ADDINGTON 76-71 |
| 1938 | F.C.ROE 74 | 1987 | G.P.ADDINGTON 72-79 |
| 1939 | C.S.CATLOW 70 | 1988 | M.BRITTEN 80-75 |
| 1940 | F.C.ROE | 1989 | A.J.CARTER 74-71* |
| 1941 | F.C.ROE 76 | 1990 | M.J.IZZARD 76-72 |
| 1942 | W.H.ABBOTT | 1991 | M.J.IZZARD 75-77 |
| 1943 | A.S.ALIBONE | 1992 | G.H.KEATES 72-77 |
| 1944 | C.S.CATLOW 77 | 1993 | D.J.JESSUP 76-76 |
| 1945 | F.C.ROE 70 | 1994 | G.H.KEATES 75-75 |
| 1946 | C.S.CATLOW | 1995 | G.H.KEATES 72-73 |
| 1947 | F.C.ROE 150-0=150 | 1996 | G.H.KEATES 72-71 |
| 1948 | J.W.TAYLOR | 1997 | J.M.LLOYD 71-70 |
| 1949 | G.F.TAYLOR | 1998 | A.J.LIMBERT 75-73* |
| 1950 | J.W.TAYLOR | 1999 | S.P.TOOTELL 73-74 |
| 1951 | J.W.TAYLOR | 2000 | G.H.KEATES 70-76 |
| 1952 | J.W.TAYLOR | 2001 | G.H.KEATES 70-69 |
| 1953 | J.W.TAYLOR | | |

* Following a 36- or 18 hole play-off, runners up:
1954 R.S.Mumford (168,36)
1962 R.G.Halliday (18)
1985 D.A.Dare (18)
1989 M.J.Izzard (18)
1998 A.J.Carter (18)

"Victory is everything. You can spend the money, but you can never spend the memories"

Ken Venturi

*Six times Club champion. Glenn Keates – 1992, 1994-6, 2000 and 2001.*

# CHAPTER 2

# AUTUMN SCRATCHCUP/MATCHPLAY CHAMPIONSHIP

"The more I practice the luckier I get."
Gary Player

THERE are many players who argue from a traditional view, that match play is the true game of amateur golf rather than the American-style medal play which has become a false norm as player numbers have grown. It could be argued that in modern times, this trophy is more difficult to win since one has to qualify for the event through the Club Championship. Neither argument on the relative difficulties of the two competitions stands up to a scientifically rigorous analysis so we must leave the final decision to equity!

Frank Hill and C.M. Phipps originally presented this trophy in October 1901 for the best score over eighteen holes in the Thursday, Saturday or Sunday rounds of the autumn meeting. The format of this event was changed to the Matchplay Championship in 1974 where one simply entered the competition with a single figure handicap, which culminated in a 36-hole final. Since 1990 those players who were the top sixteen in the club medal championship have played off for this major trophy. The format was changed in 2001 such that the top sixteen from the club championship play each other, 1vs16, 2vs15, 3vs14 etc during August and September culminating in a 36 hole final.

The first winner of the Match Play trophy was Chris Westall in 1974 who was and still is a superb ball striker and won many club trophies as a young man. He left the area for about ten years although recently we have seen his attacking swing at the club on a green fee.

*Gary Player at the Millennium Open St. Andrews
needing a lift from his caddie.*

The results show that a player often has to lose in the final once or twice before eventually lifting the trophy. This has certainly been the case for Jeremy Shepherd, Andy Limbert and Simon Tootell who have along with Dominic Jessup and Glenn Keates featured strongly in the last ten years. Interestingly since 1974 the trophy has only been won four times by players without County golf experience, which demonstrates the qualities required to capture this premier trophy.

Sadly many golfers have worked hard to get into the final only to be defeated at the last hurdle, there can be a lot of sadness in matchplay where games have been lost on for example the last, twentieth and thirty seventh holes. As a mark of respect to these players I have included their names in the results section, since runner up in such a competition means that the player was one of the best players in the Club that year. I can vividly remember three putting the thirty sixth hole at Kettering Road to eventually lose on the thirty seventh to John Smith in 1981! It felt even worse since I was actually two down with four to play and one up playing the last. I was so angry and frustrated at not being able to do what I knew I was capable of and had to wait a year to get the trophy back. That is golf! As Tony Jacklin once stated, "the more that you play the more things will happen to you" and if you have a long competitive career, you will experience all the high points and all the low points. This green was always a tough test due to the slopes and shape of the green, especially when the pin was on the top level at the back of the green.

Looking back, I should not have been surprised since I was mentally recovering from my first wife Jane's death in late 1979, perhaps my choice of caddy in new fiancée Yolanda was not a wise golfing choice. It was a great choice really since I was "allowed" to play in the 1983 Hollingsworth final the day after our wedding and before the honeymoon!

David Dare also experienced the pain of losing in the final and losing the play-off for the club championship on that fateful weekend back in 1985. Mike Lynch partially describes the story as headlines on the back page of the *Chronicle and Echo* "Who dares loses-twice, Sad David's out of luck....." County second team player, Alan Linney was crowned the champion of Northampton Golf Club when he comfortably beat David Dare in a very one-sided "grudge" 18-hole play-off for the title.

In fact it proved to be one of the most embarrassing matches in the Championship's 11-year history with the game ending, for all purposes at the second hole. After the exchange of heated words on the rules of golf following the pair's challenge for the title in late August the gallery, the largest seen attending such a club fixture, believed the final would produce some skilful and devastating golf.

But alas this was not to be. David was not actively involved in the match from the time he struggled to a nine on the second hole. Linney eventually beating Dare with a score of 73 gross. David and Mike have never yet relaxed in each other's company. Linney's caddie for the final was his county second teammate author. The pair collected the major trophies at N.G.C. when the caddying roles were reversed for the club's match play championship. Izzard was fortunate to beat a David Dare by one hole as the author's nerve held firm with a winning 36th hole bogey making David's weekend one he would like to forget.

Despite the happenings of that weekend David won many friends by the way he conducted himself in the face of adversity. The origin of the information for the Chronicle and Echo article originating from an avid Everton F.C. supporter. David "He who Dares" was to become a hero in 1988 as he played the winning shot to win the semi final of the Hollingsworth Trophy. David has such a winning desire, which has become the envy of many players. Once known affectionately as the fourteen handicapper's hero, he simply will not give up on a bad score and chases it down for respect. A simple lesson to us all.

New Club members have often surprised the established players by winning the trophy when John Costin, Peter Rees and John Varco "stole" the trophy in 1976, 1986 and 1996 respectively. Gavin Riddall became the first player to win the trophy on the new course at Harlestone in 1990 when he was "given the trophy" on the 19th after Jeremy Shepherd missed from two feet for victory on the 18th.

Between 1990 and the Millennium the trophy has been won be a wide variety of players which may possibly suggest that the new format only identifies the best player on that weekend. It would be interesting to see what results would emerge if the Club reverted back to its old format. However we need to temper such thoughts with the realisation that as the game has changed with the new technology in the form of balls, irons, spin wedges and long distance drivers can actually mean new golfers. In the last ten years there are a breed of amateurs and professionals who have significantly benefited from these developments. This is largely as a result of a player's ability to practice and also the improved methods of teaching via video and informed analysis of the simple mechanics of the golf swing. Certain individuals cannot accept that their success may simply be equipment and money given. If one analyses their real commitment to the Club's performance, one can rapidly observe that a night at a nightclub until 3 a.m. is not conducive to a clear mind the following day. A fine performance, I am convinced, would be produced if they went to bed at a suitable hour with a belly full of beer from the Club and retire early with a good golf book!

This was certainly not the behaviour displayed by Andy Limbert who made his young family proud in 1999 by finally winning the trophy. The Millennium final was watched unfortunately by a small crowd who witnessed some superb golf. This final over eighteen holes including no less than ten birdies in a wonderful contest. Simon Tootell eventually triumphing over fellow County team player Glenn Keates with a score of five under par at the seventeenth and a two and one winner at the third attempt. The 2001 final was Simon Tootell's fourth in succession where he eventually beat Jon Lloyd in a closely fought match 2 up over 36 holes in the competition's new format. Simon saved his best golf for the afternoon; going round in 69 shots three under par to turn a one-hole deficit at lunch to eventual victory.

*Simon Tootell, four times Matchplay finalist and winner 2000, 2001.*

# Autumn Scratch Cup/Matchplay Championship

| YEAR | WINNER | YEAR | WINNER | RUNNER UP |
|------|--------|------|--------|-----------|
| 1901 | N.DAWSON | 1960 | R.G.HALLIDAY | |
| 1902 | H.H.O.COOKSON 89 | 1961 | R.G.HALLIDAY 72 | |
| 1903 | N.DAWSON 84 | 1962 | R.G.HALLIDAY 76* | |
| 1904 | D.C.SCROGGIE | 1963 | R.G.HALLIDAY 75 | |
| 1905 | N.DAWSON 85 | 1964 | R.G.AITKEN | |
| 1906 | H.C.BOYCOTT 86 | 1965 | H.OLLERTON | |
| 1907 | H.C.BOYCOTT 86 | 1966 | J.M.PETTIGREW | |
| 1908 | H.C.BOYCOTT 82 | 1967 | H.R.BEIRNE | |
| 1909 | H.S.SNELL 88 | 1968 | J.M.PETTIGREW | |
| 1910 | H.S.SNELL 83 | 1969 | C.R.CIESLEWICZ | |
| 1911 | J.H.C.DAWES 92 | 1970 | A.J.PARKER | |
| 1912 | H.ALSOP 89 | 1971 | R.NEWMAN | |
| 1913 | J.H.C.DAWES 86 | 1972 | J.D.PRITCHARD | |
| 1914 | WORLD WAR | 1973 | J.M.PETTIGREW | |
|      | YEARS | 1974❏ | C.S.WESTALL | |
| 1920 | R.L.CARTWRIGHT 76 | 1975 | M.J.IZZARD 3/2 | *T.J.LUDLOW* |
| 1921 | P.D.RIDDALL 80 | 1976 | J.A.COSTIN | |
| 1922 | P.D.RIDDALL | 1977 | J.A.COSTIN 8/7 | *M.J.IZZARD* |
| 1923 | P.D.RIDDALL | 1978 | W.A.CLARKE 2/1 | *M.J.IZZARD* |
| 1924 | H.J.D.ARKELL 78 | 1979 | M.J.IZZARD 7/6 | *R.RAGBIR* |
| 1925 | D.DEMPSTER 83 | 1980 | M.J.IZZARD 6/5 | *A.J.PARKER* |
| 1926 | R.S.JELLEYMAN | 1981 | J.L.SMITH 37th | *M.J.IZZARD* |
| 1927 | O.J.HARGRAVE 75 | 1982 | M.J.IZZARD 3/2 | *A.J.LINNEY* |
| 1928 | J.DUNLOP 76 | 1983 | A.J.PARKER 3/2 | *N.DURANT* |
| 1929 | L.W.WILD 82* | 1984 | R.J.C.KILLIP 1up | *M.J.IZZARD* |
| 1930 | F.C.ROE 78 | 1985 | M.J.IZZARD 1 up | *D.A.DARE* |
| 1931 | N.W.DUNN 75 | 1986 | P.M.H.REES 2/1 | *A.J.PARKER* |
| 1932 | F.C.ROE 75 | 1987 | M.J.IZZARD 2/1 | *G.P.ADDINGTON* |
| 1933 | F.C.ROE | 1988 | M.J.IZZARD 7/6 | *G.P.ADDINGTON* |
| 1934 | F.C.ROE 79 | 1989 | D.J.JESSUP 7/6 | *A.J.CARTER* |
| 1935 | C.S.CATLOW 70 | 1990 + | G.J.RIDDALL 1up | *J.SHEPHERD* |
| 1936 | G.W.MINNEY | 1991 | A.J.PARKER 1 up | *D.J.JESSUP* |
| 1937 | R.S.JELLYMAN | 1992 | M.J.IZZARD 5/4 | *J.SHEPHERD* |
| 1938 | F.C.ROE* | 1993 | D.J.JESSUP 2/1 | *M.J.IZZARD* |
| 1939 | F.C.ROE | 1994 | J.SHEPHERD 3/2 | *G.H.KEATES* |
| 1940 | F.C.ROE | 1995 | G.H.KEATES 3/2 | *D.J.JESSUP* |
| 1941 | C.S.CATLOW | 1996 | J.J.VARCO 2/1 | *A.J.LIMBERT* |
| 1942 | C.S.CATLOW | 1997 | G.H.KEATES 1up | *A.J.LIMBERT* |
| 1943 | A.S.ALIBONE | 1998 | G.H.KEATES 3/2 | *S.P.TOOTELL* |
| 1944 | A.S.ALIBONE 71* | 1999 | A.J.LIMBERT 2/1 | *S.P.TOOTELL* |
| 1945 | G.H.WILD 74 | 2000 | S.P.TOOTELL 2/1 | *G.H.KEATES* |
| 1946 | F.C.ROE 76 | 2001# | S.P.TOOTELL 2up | *J.LLOYD* |
| 1947 | W.H.ABBOT | 2002 | | |
| 1948 | F.C.ROE | 2003 | | |

| | | |
|---|---|---|
| 1949 | J.F.MITCHELL | 2004 |
| 1950 | J.W.TAYLOR | 2005 |
| 1951 | J.W.TAYLOR | 2006 |
| 1952 | J.W.TAYLOR | 2007 |
| 1953 | E.COKER | 2008 |
| 1954 | D.C.SOUTHEY 78 | 2009 |
| 1955 | B.COOKSLEY | 2010 |
| 1956 | D.C.SOUTHEY | 2011 |
| 1957 | R.G.HALLIDAY 74 | 2012 |
| 1958 | R.G.HALLIDAY 75 | 2013 |
| 1959 | D.C.SOUTHEY | 2014 |

* 1929 Play off F.C.Roe Runner Up
1938 Play off C.S.Catlow Runner Up
1944 Play off W.Cresswell Runner Up
1962 Play off H.Waterhouse Runner Up
❑ Matchplay from 1974 onwards
+ 18 hole final from 1990-2000
# 36 hole final 2001

"Why am I using a new putter? Because the last one didn't float too well."

Craig Stadler

*Harlestone House c.1880 photographed from the current car park.*

# CHAPTER 3

# Silver Salvers/ Winter Knockout

As the author's thrown golf club disappeared into the lake on the sixteenth at Harlestone "Don't worry I've got a line on it."

Rudy Ragbir 1991

**R.G.SCRIVEN, Captain in 1900 presented the trophy on the 25th November after opening a subscription for country members only. It was originally known, as the Silver Salvers but became the Winter Knockout competition in 1991. A qualifying round over eighteen holes is held prior to the committee making a draw. The original rules stated that the player retained the handicap under which he had entered the competition.**

During my years at the Club, this competition has seen many different winners largely from the lower handicap division. Perhaps their game is a little less rusty in the winter or they are more capable of coping with the difficult conditions of wind and the frozen or wet soil. As the Silver Salvers the trophy was won a record five times by Alan Parker which also included winning the trophy three times on the trot from 1975-1977. The trophy changed from being the Silver Salvers to the Winter Knockout in 1991 when Martin Harris first won it. Young gun Alex Wray had the opportunity to equal Alan's notable achievement since he managed to win the trophy in the last two years. Interestingly Alan demonstrated that a silky swing could last the rigours of time by winning the trophy for a mind-boggling sixth time in 1998. Including the two gentlemen mentioned above, the trophy has been won on two occasions by no less than fourteen players. Alex Wray became the first player to win a trophy in the new Millennium when he successfully defended the cup. A fact he constantly refers to during bar conversations! Alex's disappointment at not achieving the treble was soon lost when he travelled to Tokyo in August 2001 for the World Transplant Olympics, where he collected a monumental five gold and two bronze medals in the swimming. He is our first World Champion at the Club, a fact we are all so proud of, from this quite unassuming young man who has been through so much physically and emotionally. Alex travelled to Tokyo with his family and friend Gavin Condon and it was rather fitting that Gavin should become the 2001 champion of the Winter Knockout.

| | | | |
|---|---|---|---|
| 1900 | Rev H.E.M.SIDDALL | 1962 | J.EYTON-JONES |
| 1901 | R.A.MILLIGAN | 1963 | D.C.SOUTHEY |
| 1902 | R.A.MILLIGAN | 1964 | W.FLYNN |
| 1903 | N.DAWSON | 1965 | R.G.HALLIDAY |
| 1904 | D.C.SCROGGIE | 1966 | L.A.JOHNSON |
| 1905 | C.W.PHIPPS | 1967 | A.J.PARKER |
| 1906 | H.C.BOYCOTT | 1968 | A.J.WOOTON |
| 1907 | H.C.BOYCOTT | 1969 | A.J.PARKER |
| 1908 | E.N.BOSTOCK | 1970 | H.R.BEIRNE |
| 1909 | N.F.BOSTOCK | 1971 | J.W.HALLIWELL |
| 1910 | E.N.BOSTOCK | 1972 | J.W.HALLIWELL |
| 1911 | W.J.HULL | 1973 | F.MASSON |
| 1912 | W.J.HULL | 1974 | C.S.WESTALL |
| 1913 | A.M.TROUP | 1975 | A.J.PARKER |
| 1914 | C.G.G.SOUTAR | 1976 | A.J.PARKER |
| 1915 | C.WRIGHT | 1977 | A.J.PARKER |
| 1920 | P.D.RIDDELL | 1978 | T.J.LUDLOW |
| 1921 | A.G.R.BARTON | 1979 | P.BRAITHWAITE |
| 1922 | J.H.C.DAWES | 1980 | K.V.NEWMAN |
| 1923 | P.D.RIDDELL | 1981 | D.WILLIAMS |
| 1924 | P.D.RIDDELL | 1982 | A.J.LINNEY |
| 1925 | A.S.ALIBONE | 1983 | K.V.MORRIS |
| 1926 | A.G.BIRD | 1984 | D.J.BROADHURST |
| 1927 | J.DUNLOP | 1985 | D.A.DARE |
| 1928 | A.J.ALIBONE | 1986 | K.V.NEWMAN |
| 1929 | L.W.WILD | 1987 | I.P.ROBINS |
| 1930 | H.J.D.ARKELL | 1988 | D.E.EBORALL |
| 1931 | C.G.G.SOUTAR | 1989 | B.J.STANBRIDGE |
| 1932 | K.W.WHITWORTH | 1990 | P.J.HIRST |
| 1933 | F.C.ROE | 1991 | **NOW WINTER KNOCK OUT** |
| | | | M.R.HARRIS 3/2 |
| 1934 | F.C.WILD | 1992 | P.J.HIRST 3/2 |
| 1935 | G.W.MINNEY | 1993 | N.J.FROST |
| 1936 | C.S.CATLOW | 1994 | M.BRITTEN |
| 1937 | F.C.ROE | 1995 | G.P.ADDINGTON 2/1 |

| | | | |
|---|---|---|---|
| 1938 | A.S.ALIBONE | 1996 | D.LAIRD |
| 1939-1946 | World War 2 | 1997 | S.TYRRELL 37th |
| 1947 | T.M.ASKEW | 1998 | A.J.PARKER |
| 1948 | W.H.CHAPMAN | 1999 | A.P.WRAY 6/5 |
| 1949 | A.J.HARRISON | 2000 | A.P.WRAY 5/4 |
| 1950 | A.J.SANDERSON | 2001 | G.CONDON 5/4 |
| 1951 | M.R.CLARKE | 2002 | |
| 1952 | L.PERRIN | 2003 | |
| 1953 | S.PANTHER | 2004 | |
| 1954 | R.C.ANDERSON | 2005 | |
| 1955 | R.W.REYNOLDS | 2006 | |
| 1956 | B.COOKSLEY | 2007 | |
| 1957 | J.EYTON-JONES | 2008 | |
| 1958 | B.J.HALL | 2009 | |
| 1959 | F.A.B.HALL | 2010 | |
| 1960 | H.OLLERTON | 2011 | |
| 1961 | W.H.CHAPMAN | 2012 | |

"I know I'm getting better at golf because I'm hitting fewer spectators"

Gerald Ford

*Alan Parker six times Winter Knockout Champion with 1996 Club Captain Martyn Smith.*

*Alex Wray, Winter Knockout Champion 1999, 2000 and
World Transplant Games Champion (swimming) 2001.*

# CHAPTER 4

# SOUTAR CUP

"The person I fear most in the last two rounds is myself"

Tom Watson eight times a Major winner. Who can possibly ever forget the long iron in to Birkdale's final hole in 1983 by the man with Popeye forearms?

**C.G.G. SOUTAR presented the trophy on the 15th October in his year as Captain; it is competed for over 36 holes of medal play in the spring meeting. Gordon (C.G.G.) Soutar was made a life member in1926.**

This is one trophy that has not been dominated by any one individual. In fact, Laurie Johnson, the former Northamptonshire wicket keeper, remains the only player to have won the Soutar Cup twice (1962 and 1966). At Kettering Road players of all handicaps won the trophy whereas at Harlestone low handicappers have dominated the winners' board.

Jack Turner, the auburn hair'd relaxed "country boy" who appears to not have a care in the world won the trophy in my first year at the Club. As an impressionable Junior I could never understand how he could play so well with the club toed in by those large firm hands. Junior colleague Paul Bingham lifted the trophy from his Senior colleagues in 1973, which brought on many cries of bandit! Bob Frost won this his one and only trophy in 1977 before becoming a well-respected supporter of the Club and Captain in 1995.

Brother's Adrian and Martin Peacock won the trophy in 1985 and 1991 on the old and new courses respectively, and are probably still arguing about which was the greater victory. In 1985 Adrian won the cup with a fine score of 169–30=139. The local paper continues the story:- Thirteen year old Adrian, a Kingsthorpe Upper School pupil has added the Soutar Cup to his impressive cabinet. He's been playing for three years, now on a 15 handicap and is a regular player at the Kettering Road course. "I bike to the course as often as possible," he said this week. " I'd obviously like to become a professional but at the moment I don't know if I'll reach that stage."

His handicap rapidly reduced to 10 over the warm summer months and included a gross 72 during the qualifying stages of the Northampton Cup. Adrian's round was completed without a six on the card, which earned him some golf balls from the Sunday Express. He did not become a professional golfer in the end but became a professional engineer!

Gavin Condon's remarkable score of 127 Nett in 1997 included a course record equaling 67 gross.

*Dominic Jessup, winner of the Club's three 36-hole competitions;*
*Club Champion 1993, Soutar Cup 1999 and Stanhope Cup 2001.*

| | | | |
|---|---|---|---|
| 1927 | J.DUNLOP 173-24=149 | 1970 | J.W.HARRIS 168-40=128 |
| 1928 | H.J.D.ARKELL 157-14=143 | 1971 | G.B.PYKE 159-16=143 |
| 1929 | G.MARKIE 184-40=144 | 1972 | D.MABBUTT 171-32=139 |
| 1930 | F.C.ROE 157-16=141 | 1973 | P.BINGHAM 162-38=134 |
| 1931 | G.MARKIE 166-20=146 | 1974 | R.E.BRACKLEY 178-38=140 |
| 1932 | F.M.JONES | 1975 | J.C.HUNTER 157-14=143 |
| 1933 | G.W.MINNEY | 1976 | B.RUSSELL 160-26=134 |
| 1934 | L.BAILEY | 1977 | R.A.FROST 178-40=138 |
| 1935 | P.G.JONES | 1978 | F.A.JOHNSON 163-28=135 |
| 1936 | J.EYTON-JONES 69-67=136 | 1979 | W.BERRY 175-36=139 |
| 1937 | J.E.GIFFIN 181-36=145 | 1980 | K.THREFALL 171-36=135 |
| 1938 | A.N.SOUTAR 66-71+137 | 1981 | R.E.MONTGOMERY 174-40=134 |
| 1939 | E.COKER 177-34* | 1982 | R.G.BUSWELL 165-26=139 |
| 1940 | R.E.RUSHTON 164-20=144 | 1983 | M.THATCHER 156-24=132 |
| 1941 | A.G.HALLIDAY 90-18=72 | 1984 | R.K.DICK 162-30=132 |
| 1942 | J.P.GAINSFORD 174-34=140 | 1985 | A.J.PEACOCK169-30=139 |
| 1943 | H.C.ANDERSON 170-28=142 | 1986 | K.J.VALLANCE 71-64=135 |
| 1944 | H.W.JANISCH 85-18=67 | 1987 | D.E.EBORALL |
| 1945 | F.GARRARD 71-71=142* | 1988 | K.V.MORRIS 73-67=140* |
| 1946 | R.H.BLAIR | 1989 | T.J.PANTHER |
| 1947 | R.C.CATT | 1990 | G.H.KEATES |
| 1948 | D.J.TYRELL | 1991 | M.C.PEACOCK 67-73=140 |
| 1949 | J.H.BAXTER | 1992 | P.J.HIRST |
| 1950 | R.L.LOWERY | 1993 | C.HOPEWELL 64-74=138 |
| 1951 | D.C.SOUTHEY | 1994 | S.TYRELL |
| 1952 | R.L.CLARKE | 1995 | M.J.BLAKE |
| 1953 | P.RUSHTON | 1996 | C.P.JOHNSON |
| 1954 | R.S.MUMFORD 71-73=144 | 1997 | G.CONDON 61-66=127 |
| 1955 | B.COOKSLEY 66-70=136 | 1998 | M.C.POUND |
| 1956 | J.L.WILSON 75-72=147 | 1999 | D.JESSUP 142 |
| 1957 | A.LYON 66-69=135 | 2000 | G.S.STEWART 66-74=140 |
| 1958 | A.COKER 72-72=144 | 2001 | J.W.LLOYD 70-71=141 |
| 1959 | S.PANTHER 77+67=144 | 2002 | |
| 1960 | W.SHARP 166-24=142 | 2003 | |
| 1961 | J.M.GERARD 70-72=142 | 2004 | |
| 1962 | L.A.JOHNSON 68-64=132 | 2005 | |
| 1963 | J.T.ROUSE 68-70=141 | 2006 | |
| 1964 | W.A.CLARKE 69-68=137 | 2007 | |
| 1965 | B.W.SCOTT 75-70=145 | 2008 | |
| 1966 | L.A.JOHNSON 154-14=140 | 2009 | |
| 1967 | T.THOMPSON 155-18=137 | 2010 | |
| 1968 | W.A.CLARKE 72-66=138 | 2011 | |
| 1969 | C.J.TURNER 164-30=134 | 2012 | |

*1939 Play off  W.A.Dunn Runner Up
1945 Play off A.Coker Runner Up
1988 Play off T.Addington Runner Up

*Seve – One man who changed the face of European golf, at Woburn 1986, wearing his Open Championship jumper.*

# CHAPTER 5

# SPENCER CUP

"Golf got complicated when I had to wear shoes and think about it"

Sam Snead.

THIS TROPHY and indeed Northampton Golf Club has a long association with the Spencer family since our first president was Earl Spencer (The Red Earl) in 1893 and the new course at Harlestone was officially opened on the seventeenth of June 1991 by Viscount and Viscountess Spencer. The Red Earl was one of the original forty five founder members of Northampton G.C., some of them used to travel by horse and cart to play with members of the first Golf Club in Northamptonshire, Kettering which was established in 1891. I find it a pathetic scenario now that some pampered members of Club and County teams find it difficult to travel a relatively short distance of say eighty miles, in total air-conditioned comfort to a match. If only they new!

At the annual dinner of the Club, on the 16th November 1895 Earl Spencer presented the trophy, which was originally known as the Presidents Trophy, which is now better known as the Spencer Cup. The trophy was originally played for as an 18 hole medal but since the 1950s has been awarded to the winner of a bogey competition over eighteen holes played during the spring meeting. The original handicap limit was 24 now reduced to 20 for each competitor.

In more recent times one could not discuss the Spencer Trophy without reference to our Northamptonshire Lady, Diana Spencer. I am sure I speak for all real Northamptonians who were so proud of what Diana achieved in her short though significant life. Sunday the 31st August 1997 was a day none of us will ever forget, 24 hours that began in disbelief and ended with the gradual comprehension that an unimaginable tragedy had come to pass. I will never forget how numb the County felt on that fateful day.

This emotionally ran parallels through my mind since when I lost my first wife Jane Anne in 1979 from a brain haemorrhage I had little knowledge of how our Golf Club at Harlestone, the Spencer feelings and my emotions would be interwoven. As a young man with a relatively narrow vision of life Jane taught me the arty side of life with music by Debussy, how to appreciate Constable/Turner *et al*, and to keep an open mind. The subtle emotional themes that run through songs we enjoyed together as teenagers such as the 1971 classic Stairway to Heaven, serve as a catalytic reminder of my love for her.

## Stairway to Heaven

There's a lady who's sure all that glitters is gold
And she's buying a stairway to heaven
And when she gets there she knows
If the stores are closed
With a word she can get what she can get what she came for

There's a sign on the wall
But she wants to be sure
Cause you know words have
Two meanings
In a tree by the brook there's a songbird
Who sings sometimes
All of our thoughts are Misgiven

There's a feeling I get when I look
To the west
And my spirit is crying for leaving
In my thoughts I have seen rings of smoke
Through the trees
And the voices of those who stand looking

And it's whispered that soon if we all
Call the tune
Then the piper will lead us to reason
And a new day will dawn for those
Who stand long
And the forests will echo with Laughter
And it makes me wonder

If there's a bustle in your hedgerow
Don't be alarmed know
It's just a spring clean for the May-Queen
Yes there are two paths you can go by
But in the long run
There's still time to change the road you're on

Your head is humming and it won't go
In case you don't know
The pipers calling you to join him
Dear Lady can you hear the wind blow
And did you know
Your stairway lies on the whispering wind

Jimmy Page & Robert Plant
Atlantic Records 1971


When she died my heart was smashed in two, a scenario no one of twenty-four would look for. We used to walk over the course at Harlestone as teenagers interested in birdwatching with my mother and father long before it was ever thought of as a golf course. My late parents also used to walk around the lake as a courting couple back in the nineteen fifties and apparently enjoyed a kiss and a cuddle under a coat by the large horse chestnut tree close to the boat house. The woodpeckers and nuthatches are still present twenty-five years later together with a few new buzzards.

In 1998 whilst we were playing the semi-final of the tartan trophy with partner Glenn Keates, against Stuart McArthur and Alan West on Saturday evening the 27 June one day after my forty third birthday, I could feel the emotions being generated as the groups warmed up the fifteen thousand people gathered across the wall at Althorp House for The Tribute Concert. If you ever have a chance to watch the video recorded that evening the songs of "My lady in Red" "Climb every Mountain" and "High on Emotion" typified my feelings that evening. Sadly the narrator of the video another beautiful lady Gill Dando was murdered by some moron in London. The views of the oak trees on our course the Spencer estate mingling beautifully with the views of the house, the colourfully dressed audience, the dark green grass, the lake and stable block. As I stood upon the fifth tee with the music playing around us just before I hit my nine iron I remarked to my opponent "Poor old lady Diana" The ball travelled with a sense of eerie accuracy and finished in the bottom of the hole! At the conclusion of the game this was much to the delight of the players and those assembled in the clubhouse on Invitation Day. Divine intervention or pure concentration?

*Plaque to remember Earl Spencer's daughter, Diana, Princess of Wales.*

Watching her sons growing up, in particular William at the same rate as my son Alex is always an emotional reminder of how we were so proud of our Lady from the Shire of Spires and Squires. She had a total empathy with everyone from Aid's victims to Royalty.

## Candle in the Wind

Goodbye England's rose; may you ever grow in our hearts.
You were the grace that placed itself where lives were torn apart.
You called out to our country, and you whispered to those in pain.
Now you belong to heaven, and the stars spell out your name.

And it seems to me you lived your life like a candle in the wind:
never fading with the sunset when the rain set in.
And your footsteps will always fall here, along England's greenest hills;
your candle's burned out long before your legend ever will.

Loveliness we've lost; these empty days without a smile.
This torch we'll always carry for our nation's golden child.
And even though we try, the truth brings us to tears; all our words cannot express the joy you brought us through the years.

Goodbye England's rose, from a country lost without your sole,
who'll miss the wings of your compassion more than you'll ever know.

Rewritten words to Elton John's Candle in the Wind sung at Westminster Abbey at Diana's funeral 6 September 1997.

We look forward to seeing her memorial in the centre of the town as promised by the Council in 2001.

Returning to the Spencer trophy. Through the years it has been won mainly by low handicap players apart from interventions by past Captains Brian Frost, Trevor Lloyd, Ron Whittaker and Peter Huntley, who have carried the flag for the middle handicap players. Brian could have possibly won the trophy as a treble had he not been defeated in a play off by Tony Lane in 1981. Brian continues the story. " I could have won it four times. In my Captain's year in 1988 I was deemed to have taken four on the third hole on the old course although my ball went in for a two! The gentlemen attending the pin forgot to take the pin out. Plus one won the cup and I finished minus one as a result of the unfortunate gentlemen's action. He actually offered to take the penalty on his score card, which the committee would not allow." The winning Captain's theme being continued by Tony Stevens in 1961 and Silver Fox Ken Billingham in 1976.

The trophy has been retained on five occasions recently by Norman Jones in 1970 and by Ken Morris in 1985. In 1998 the trophy was won in a play off by popular Club character Tony (DeVito) Bason in his first year as a full member, we are still hearing about it graphically to date! In 1999 Steve Eborall scored a remarkable five up to win the cup and young Chris Hopewell restated the low handicapper's dominance the following year by became the Millennium winner.

*Club characters Bobby and Tony Bason, Dawland & Spencer Cup winners 1990 and 1998 respectively.*

| | |
|---|---|
| 1895 W.C.HENDERSON | 1957 N.JONES +5 |
| 1896 Reverend W.H.DEANE 94-12=82 | 1958 R.BEIRNE −3 |
| 1897 R.P.PHILIPS 103-18=82 | 1959 H.OLLERTON allsqr |
| 1898 D.P.TAYLOR | 1960 W.L.WATSON-1 |
| 1899 F.HILL | 1961 A.F.STEVENS +2 |
| 1900 R.A.MILLIGAN 95-11=84 | 1962 J.M.GERARD +1 |
| 1901 H.N.SMITH 95-14=81 | 1963 S.PANTHER −1* |
| 1902 H.N.SMITH 93-9=84 | 1964 L.A.JOHNSON allsqr* |
| 1903 N.DAWSON 84-3=81 | 1965 R.RUFFELL −1 |
| 1904 H.ALSOP | 1966 J.T.CIESLEWICZ −2 |
| 1905 E.H.LANKESTER 96-16=80 | 1967 H.A.MILNER −1 |
| 1906 H.C.BOYCOTT 86-5=81 | 1968 J.T.CIESLEWICZ −1 |
| 1907 J.F.STOPS 91-11=80 | 1969 N.JONES +2 |
| 1908 H.C.BOYCOTT 82-3=79 | 1970 N.JONES +2 |
| 1909 H.S.SNELL 87-8=79 | 1971 R.I.BOTWOOD +2 |
| 1910 H.S.SNELL 83-8=75 | 1972 P.GRAHAM allsqr |
| 1911 C.WRIGHT 94-12=82 | 1973 R.E.MILES +5 |
| 1912 S.B.TAYLOR 89-16=73 | 1974 M.J.BUTLER +2 |
| 1913 J.H.G.DAWES 87-8=79 | 1975 J.TRAHEARN −2* |
| 1920 R.N.CHURCH 92-14=78 | 1976 K.BILLINGHAM −1 |
| 1921 J.H.G.DAWES 87-6=81 | 1977 T.J.LUDLOW +2 |
| 1922 T.R.TAYLOR | 1978 L.A.JAMES -3 |
| 1923 P.H.BUNTING 90-14=76 | 1979 A.F.STEVENS allsqr |
| 1924 P.D.RIDDELL 82-2=80 | 1980 B.J.FROST +2* |
| 1925 D.DEMPSTER 83-7=76 | 1981 A.LANE −4* |
| 1926 C.G.G.SOUTAR 82-8=74 | 1982 B.J.FROST +1 |
| 1927 G.B.MUSCOTT 81-7=74 | 1983 D.EVANS −2 |
| 1928 L.W.WILD 79-5=74 | 1984 K.V.MORRIS −1 |
| 1929 F.C.ROE 85-11=74 | 1985 K.V.MORRIS allsqr |
| 1930 F.C.ROE 78-6=72 | 1986 R.W.RIDDALL +3 |
| 1931 P.G.JONES 77-8=69 | 1987 T.J.LLOYD =1 |
| 1932 F.C.ROE 75-1=74 | 1988 K.HEARD allsqr* |
| 1933 K.C.WHITLOCK 70 | 1989 R.WALTON |
| 1934 J.WILLIAMSON 86-16=70 | 1990 T.W.WILSON |
| 1935 J.S.DAVIDSON 86-12=76 | 1991 R.W.WHITTAKER |
| 1936 S.N.HILL 86-18=68 | 1992 J.SHEPHERD |
| 1937 P.HUTTON 76-8=68 | 1993 A.STENSONES +3 |
| 1938 J.H.MILLS 80-12=68 | 1994 P.R.HUNTLEY +5 |
| 1939 E.A.WOOD 86-18=68 | 1995 T.J.LUDLOW +4 |
| 1940 F.ALIBONE 78-6=72 | 1996 G.D.CASTLE |
| 1941 F.G.WATTS | 1997 S.EBORALL |
| 1942 E.S.BUTLIN 90-18=72 | 1998 A.R.BASON |
| 1943 H.G.SHEPPARD 85-13=72 | 1999 I.A.DAKIN |
| 1944 T.A.JEYES 81-12=69* | 2000 C.R.HOPEWELL +4 |
| 1945 R.BREWSTER 87-14=73* | 2001 S.F.BOADEN +6 |

| | | |
|---|---|---|
| 1946 | W.EYTON-JONES 85-16=79 | 2002 |
| 1947 | E.G.HARLEY | 2003 |
| 1948 | H.J.SHENFIELD | 2004 |
| 1949 | S.J.MORTON | 2005 |
| 1950 | C.C.WESTON | 2006 |
| 1951 | A.PROCTOR | 2007 |
| 1952 | H.S.WHITE | 2008 |
| 1953 | W.K.HUNTER | 2009 |
| 1954 | F.BONHAM -3 | 2010 |
| 1955 | A.J.TYRELL allsqr | 2011 |
| 1956 | S.PANTHER +1* | 2012 |

*1944 Play off R.G.Halliday Runner Up
1945 Play off W.H.Abbott Runner Up
1956 Play off M.R.Clarke Runner Up
1963 Play off J.Eyton-Jones, J.D.McNamara, E.C.Odds, A.Trahearn, M.Curwood Runners Up
1964 Play off N.D.Jones Runner Up
1975 Play off J.D.Pritchard Runner Up
1980 Play off R.W.Riddall Runner Up
1981 Play off B.J.Frost Runner Up
1988 Play off R.K.Dick Runner Up

"The only treasure in the life we live, is in a measure of the love we give
All that matters in end will be, the love in you and the love in me
That's all that matters"

Cliff Richard

# CHAPTER 6

# CORONATION or THURSDAY CUP

"What other people find in poetry, I find in the flight of a good drive."

Arnold Palmer.

**IN 1938 the committee decided to award this trophy to the winner in the final played off between the winners of the 6 medal competitions held on Thursday in alternative months. Owing to a decline in numbers it was subsequently played for on one Thursday in an eighteen-hole medal competition. From 1938-1952 it was known as the Thursday Cup but became the Coronation Cup in 1953 when her Majesty Queen Elizabeth II was crowned. Her Majesty the Queen is the Patron of the English Golf Union, the governing body of Amateur golf. Since 1953 the trophy has been awarded to the winner of an eighteen-hole Stableford competition played during the spring meeting.**

Through the early years the trophy has been defended three times, however in this book's focus, many developing golfers have won the trophy. From 1973 onwards it is interesting to note the number of young players who have lifted this trophy. Paul (bandit) Bingham continued his winning weekend streak by lifting this and the Soutar Cup in 1973. This was followed by another junior win in 1975 when young Glenn Cottrell lifted the trophy. Mark (Brain of) Britten, Gary (Pellet) Addington and Adrian (Magoo) Peacock between 1983-1992 were continuing the Junior theme. All of these young players were to become first team players and valued members of the Scratch and Hollingsworth teams.

In 1987 Brian Page lifted the trophy despite stating on the tenth tee on a freezing day. "I would rather be at home painting." Young Adam Stevens son of the often misunderstood though great supporter of golf and past

N.G.U. President featured in the winners circle in 1994. Gavin Condon finished the young winner scenario as millennium winner. There have also been many young at heart winners, whose names temporarily escape me although Alan Linney should be probably cited in this context.

*Alan Linney, Coronation Cup winner 1977*

| Year | Name | | Year | Name |
|------|------|---|------|------|
| 1938 | M.JONES 94-18=76 | | 1975 | G.R.COTTRELL 37 pts |
| 1939 | F.C.ROE 72-0=72 | | 1976 | G.HANTS 39 pts |
| 1940 | C.S.CATLOW 78+1=79 | | 1977 | A.J.LINNEY 40 pts |
| 1941 | L.J.T.R.BIRD 87-17=70 | | 1978 | R.BEIRNE 35 pts* |
| 1942 | W.T.RUSSELL 91-21=70 | | 1979 | M.HARRIS 38 pts |
| 1943 | A.G.HALLIDAY | | 1980 | A.ANDRES 40 pts |
| 1944 | A.G.HALLIDAY 84-10=74 | | 1981 | D.EVANS 34 pts |
| 1945 | T.A.JEYES 78-6=72 | | 1982 | F.A.JOHNSON 38 pts |
| 1946 | E.COKER 80-7=73 | | 1983 | R.HOLDING 37 pts* |
| 1947 | A.J.HARRISON | | 1984 | J.R.HILL 37 pts |
| 1948 | A.J.SAUNDERSON | | 1985 | A.FAIRLESS 37 pts |
| 1949 | S.J.LOVELL | | 1986 | R.W.RIDDALL 44 pts |
| 1950 | R.L.LOWERY | | 1987 | B.PAGE 37 pts |
| 1951 | R.L.LOWERY | | 1988 | M.BRITTEN 37 pts |
| 1952 | A.E.TEASDALE | | 1989 | D.J.HOLDING |
| 1953 | R.G.ANDERSON* | | 1990 | A.WHITMORE |
| 1954 | D.F.ROBINSON 33pts | | 1991 | G.P.ADDINGTON 37 pts |
| 1955 | R.L.LOWERY 36pts | | 1992 | A.J.PEACOCK |
| 1956 | R.G.HALLIDAY 39 pts | | 1993 | S.L.McARTHUR 38 pts |
| 1957 | A.LYON 38 pts | | 1994 | A.D.STEVENS 41 pts |
| 1958 | R.BEIRNE 40 pts | | 1995 | K.FAREY |
| 1959 | B.J.HALL 36 pts | | 1996 | M.J.POUND |
| 1960 | D.C.SOUTHEY 42 pts | | 1997 | P.BEEBY |
| 1961 | D.C.SOUTHEY 36 pts | | 1998 | D.H.SMITH |
| 1962 | P.BAMENT 41 pts | | 1999 | R.BARTLETT |
| 1963 | S.PANTHER 39 pts | | 2000 | G.CONDON 41 pts |
| 1964 | N.A.HAVART 38 pts | | 2001 | P.A.NOBLE 39 pts |
| 1965 | M.CURWEN 35 pts | | 2002 | |
| 1966 | J.A.SALE 39 pts | | 2003 | |
| 1967 | R.MATTHEWS 34 pts* | | 2004 | |
| 1968 | C.C.WESTON 39 pts | | 2005 | |
| 1969 | J.W.EASON 39 pts | | 2006 | |
| 1970 | D.H.CLARKE 39 pts | | 2007 | |
| 1971 | G.D.COLES 40 pts | | 2008 | |
| 1972 | J.A.SALE 38 pts | | 2009 | |
| 1973 | P.BINGHAM 44 pts | | 2010 | |
| 1974 | J.CROY 39 pts | | 2011 | |

*1967 Play off W.Clarke Runner Up
1978 Play off B.J.Frost Runner Up
1983 Play off Runners up R.Ragbir & T.Wallburton

*The steps we take against the flow may be hard but often bring a brighter future.*

# CHAPTER 7

# Rabbits Cup

"A golfer rarely needs to hit a spectacular shot unless the one that precedes it was pretty bad"

Harvey Penick

**PRESENTED by S.Colman in 1956 this trophy is played as an eighteen-hole medal competition limited to handicap of originally twenty now twenty-one.**

There have been few young winners of this trophy apart from Ian Oliver, Adam Stevens and Terry Addington in 1984, 1992 and 1995 respectively. Nicely, many well-known players such as Bill Berry, Jack Bird the Seniors Organiser, have won the trophy for many years and Alf Bond in 1973, 1982 and 1987. Bob Wiseman in recent times has been the only player to win the trophy on two occasions following in the past by Bell Fruit Machine giant Jack Shine and Derek Wills. Jack moved away from the club in the seventies to become a member of Church Brampton, however he still remained a great supporter of our club. The last time I saw him was on the eighteenth hole at Valderrama at the Volvo Masters in 1990 when he was genuinely interested in how the Club had developed especially with the move to Harlestone. I confirmed that we are now in a settled mode and looking to become recognised regionally as one of Northamptonshire's best courses.

Gil Sibley author of the centenary history book and long time member recorded his only trophy victory in 1968. The sixty barrier was broken in 1984 when Ian Oliver recorded a remarkable score of 59 ten under par to win the trophy by a mile. The Millennium winner was eventually Terry Addington following a tie with young and very promising Darren Mattacola. Terry becoming the three times winner in 2001, having defended the trophy.

| | |
|---|---|
| 1956 A.F.HERITAGE 100-27=73 | 1984 I.OLIVER 80-21=59 |
| 1957 J.SHINE 95-24=71 | 1985 D.H.SMITH 84-23=61 |
| 1958 J.SHINE 95-22=73 | 1986 A.R.WISEMAN 66 |
| 1959 N.C.TOULSON 89-23=66 | 1987 A.W.BOND 88-23=65 |
| 1960 N.A.HAVANT 92-23=69 | 1988 R.PUGH 85-23=62 |
| 1961 E.J.BAKER 82-23=59 | 1989 R.R.CARTER |
| 1962 D.T.WOOD 81-24=57 | 1990 A.G.WEBB |
| 1963 D.WILLS 89-24=65 | 1991 G.FITZWILLIAMS 91-21=70 |
| 1964 D.WILLS 68# | 1992 A.D.STEVENS |
| 1965 R.M.BILLINGTON 91-22=69 | 1993 A.R.WISEMAN 91-23=68 |
| 1966 Jas.ROUSE 90-22=68 | 1994 J.B.GILL 97-26=71 |
| 1967 S.PRAGNELL 90-24=66 | 1995 T.M.ADDINGTON 99-28=71 |
| 1968 G.SIBLEY 89-24=65 | 1996 F.SALISBURY |
| 1969 R.G.SOANES 86-22=64 | 1997 A.M.HUGHES |
| 1970 G.TIPPING | 1998 A.FINDLEY |
| 1971 K.TAYLOR 89-22=67 | 1999 P.D.DAISLEY |
| 1972 A.E.RICHARDS 87-20=67* | 2000 T.M.ADDINGTON 88-20=68 |
| 1973 W.H.BERRY 87-20=67 | 2001 T.M.ADDINGTON 95-20=75 |
| 1974 R.A.LAY 87-22=65 | 2002 |
| 1975 A.J.VINCENT 87-24=63 | 2003 |
| 1976 B.E.SHAW 88-22=66 | 2004 |
| 1977 P.B.COULSON 90-20=70 | 2005 |
| 1978 P.J.THOMPSON 88-24=64 | 2006 |
| 1979 G.R.ASHTON 91-20=71* | 2007 |
| 1980 R.SWIFT 93-24=69* | 2008 |
| 1981 M.F.A.SPICER 92-24=68 | 2009 |
| 1982 J.D.BIRD 86-21=65 | 2010 |
| 1983 J.G.W.HARMAN 90-23=67 | 2011 |
| | 2012 |

# Record book says E.Jewitt 86-23=63?
*Play Off
1972 L.H.Ridd Runner Up
1979 D.B.Pilkington & A.J.Sabin RUs
1980 S.Yule & S.A.Pollard RUs

# CHAPTER 8

# Veterans Cup

"Like the classic plays and symphonies Sam Snead doesn't belong to just one generation. His mark will be left on golf for eternity

Peter Thompson

**THE TROPHY was presented by Mr. J.Meacock in 1954 to be played for annually as an 18 hole medal competition and open to members whose age shall exceed fifty eight on the 1st January of the year of the competition. This age limit was reduced to fifty-five in July 1959 due to a lack on entries.**

Although I only briefly knew Bill Hollingsworth as a young man, without my current knowledge of tradition, it is wonderful to see such a great supporter of golf's name on this trophy as the inaugural winner. My grandfather ran a bakery shop in Abington Avenue (Faulkner's Bakery) where he used to come in for what was called a split top loaf. Only nine players entered the competition that year at an entry fee of two bob. Bill Hollingsworth picked up eighteen shillings as a prize on the sweep but would have been more pleased with the trophy than any financial reward.

Sam Clements, Ron Trigg, Eric Rouse, Brian Ager and Fred Perkins have lifted the trophy on two occasions. Eric Rouse in 1979&80 and Frank Sketchley in 1960&1 have both retained the trophy.

Ray Moir lifted the trophy in 1996 since the Club's fruit machine had broken down and he played golf for a change!

The winning score has been nett 62 on three occasions in 1972, 1983 and the Millennium winner the well known window cleaner "Fffing" Frank Bustin who climbed down his ladder to win comfortably. He was proud to receive the trophy on trophies night with the boys and close friend Club Captain Tony Harrison singing "When I'm cleaning Windows". He does not look old enough to be a Veteran!

*Sam Snead, aged 88, dancing on the 800-year-old Swilken bridge at the Millennium Open St. Andrews.*

| | | | |
|---|---|---|---|
| 1954 | W.HOLLINGSWORTH 99-24=75 | 1984 | L.P.CLARKE 79-15=64 |
| 1955 | N.H.LEWIS 96-20=76 | 1985 | R.WILLINGHAM 83-16=67 |
| 1956 | F.E.WIGMORE 92-24=68 | 1986 | E.J.GORDON 81-18=63 |
| 1957 | C.B.THOMPSON 90-24=66 | 1987 | K.T.PAUL 92-27=85 |
| 1958 | F.RIDDICK 89-16=73 | 1988 | H.S.ROAKE 96-28=68* |
| 1959 | A.J.TYRRELL 91-18=73 | 1989 | D.A.WEST |
| 1960 | F.SKETCHLEY 90-16=74 | 1990 | F.A.JOHNSON |
| 1961 | F.SKETCHLEY 83-17=66 | 1991 | W.T.EALES 70 |
| 1962 | V.G.MANN 91-20=71 | 1992 | R.S.CHERRY |
| 1963 | M.S.FLOYD 83-15=68 | 1993 | C.BRIDGEWATER 86-18=68 |
| 1964 | V.S.MANN 88-21=67 | 1994 | F.C.PERKINS 93-22=71 |
| 1965 | C.HOWKINS 85-12=73 | 1995 | B.J.AGER 86-20=66 |
| 1966 | M.S.FLOYD 86-15=71 | 1996 | A.R.MOIR |
| 1967 | L.G.HASDELL 93-23=70 | 1997 | B.J.AGER |
| 1968 | E.JEWITT 93-22=71 | 1998 | W.L.MORRIS |
| 1969 | H.S.GARDINER 92-24=68* | 1999 | F.C.PERKINS |
| 1970 | A.CLEMENTS 80-13=67 | 2000 | F.BUSTIN |
| 1971 | R.V.TRIGG 85-17=68 | 2001 | M.M.WOODS 85-17=68 |
| 1972 | A.CLEMENTS 75-13=62 | 2002 | |
| 1973 | J.NEEDHAM 84-18=66 | 2003 | |
| 1974 | R.L.CLARKE 86-16=70 | 2004 | |
| 1975 | R.V.TRIGG 88-19=69 | 2005 | |
| 1976 | D.C.SOUTHEY 77-11=66 | 2006 | |
| 1977 | C.J.BRYDON 79-10=69 | 2007 | |
| 1978 | C.C.WESTON 82-12=70 | 2008 | |
| 1979 | E.ROUSE 86-16=70 | 2009 | |
| 1980 | E.ROUSE 85-15=70* | 2010 | |
| 1981 | F.C.REBMAN 84-18=66 | 2011 | |
| 1982 | J.A.BRAZIER 86-20=66 | 2012 | |
| 1983 | S.A.POLLARD 83-21=62 | 2013 | |

*Play Off 1969 A.C.Trahearn Runner Up
1980 L.Richardson RU
1985 L.P.Clarke, F.Hodges & C.J.Turner RU's
1988 I.J.Griffiths RU

*Onion Spinney at the back of the seventeenth hole, prior to the trees being removed as part of the natural woodland cycle.*

# CHAPTER 9

# Frank Wild Cup

"Middle age is when a broad mind and a narrow waist exchange places"

Anon

**F.C. WILD (Captain 1933 and former competition secretary) presented this trophy in 1943. The committee decided to award it on the results of an 18 holes medal with a handicap limit of twenty played for by 3 finalists who qualified as follows. Two 18 hole medal rounds will be played one on Thursday, one on Saturday. The winner on Thursday, and the winner and runner up on the Saturday shall play in the final on a date fixed by the committee. This trophy is now presented to the winner of an eighteen-hole handicap competition, played on the Thursday and Saturday of the autumn meeting still with a handicap limit of twenty.**

In this book's focus the trophy has only been won twice by John Petts in 1997 and in the Millennium year. A low score of Nett 60 at Kettering Road was recorded by Brian Meadows in 1975 which was eclipsed by the remarkable score of nett 58 gross 73 by young Tony Addington in 1988. This score was achieved with a brand new set of Mizuno Domino irons, which Tony had just been given as a twenty first birthday present. His handicap was suitably adjusted! As in previous trophies the young lad's winning theme was continued by Scott Bailey, Martin Peacock and Ian Hedges in 1990,1992 and 1995.

There have been a few 61s scored several 62s and many 63s recorded over the years, with an average winning score of 65 to win this attractive trophy.

In purely numerical terms it is wise and logical to have separate divisions for medal play in an attempt to generate a level playing field. A player with a handicap of five is not likely to score more than five under par, since the difference in absolute playing ability between a five and scratch handicap is huge. A player with a twenty-eight handicap could relatively easily score five under since the absolute difference between a twenty-eight and a twenty-three handicap is not that great. Such are the thoughts raised by the handicap scheme. This trophy does not have divisions. Interestingly players having handicaps between six and twelve have won the trophy quite often. This possibly reflects that when they do play well they have sufficient relative handicap advantage to stretch them away from the field. The trophy has also been won quite often by high handicap players since when they do have a good day none of the low men can get anywhere near them.

It is nice to see such trophies being spread among players of differing ability. The aim of every member is to have their name on a trophy board and to feel proud of their achievement every time they have a sneaky look!

| | | | |
|---|---|---|---|
| 1944 | A.COKER 85-12=73 | 1979 | S.BLACKAMORE 81-15=66* |
| 1945 | H.E.LACY 87-16=71 | 1980 | A.BOWEN* 80-12=68 |
| 1946 | E.COKER 79-7=72 | 1981 | J.R.DYSON 80-19=61 |
| 1947 | A.J.HARRISON | 1982 | P.BARRETT 74-10=64 |
| 1948 | H.S.WHITE | 1983 | H.McROBERTS 79-15=64* |
| 1949 | A.F.TEASDALE | 1984 | K.BONHAM 80-18=62* |
| 1950 | M.R.CLARKE | 1985 | M.THATCHER 71-9=62 |
| 1951 | W.CRAIG | 1986 | R.SOLOMAN 81-18=63 |
| 1952 | H.J.SHENFIELD | 1987 | J.A.GRAHAM 79-15=64 |
| 1953 | D.G.ROBERTS | 1988 | T.R.ADDINGTON 73-15=58 |
| 1954 | J.H.M.GREEN 80-12=68 | 1989 | B.O'CONNELL |
| 1955 | W.H.CHAPMAN 91-19=72* | 1990 | S.BAILEY |
| 1956 | R.BEIRNE 91-17=74 | 1991 | J.T.KELLY 78-15=63 |
| 1957 | W.J.BARRON 92-24=68 | 1992 | M.PEACOCK 78-10=68 |
| 1958 | N.JONES 76-5=71 | 1993 | E.W.MARRIS 85-20 |
| 1959 | R.BEIRNE 81-14=67 | 1994 | J.MUNNS |
| 1960 | J.SHINE 89-19=70 | 1995 | I.R.HEDGES 80-19=61 |
| 1961 | E.F.FULLER 80-15=65 | 1996 | Sir D.J.O'DOWD |
| 1962 | W.G.BOTWOOD 85-18=67 | 1997 | J.W.PETTS |
| 1963 | G.B.PYKE 86-18=68 | 1998 | D.J.WEBSTER |
| 1964 | N.D.JONES 80-12=68 * | 1999 | R.BAKER |
| 1965 | B.W.E.PEOPLE 85-15=70* | 2000 | J.W.PETTS 74-8=66 |
| 1966 | P.ST.QUINTON 75-8=67 | 2001 | P.BOWEN 79-15=64 |
| 1967 | D.C.HODDER 79-13=66 | 2002 | |
| 1968 | H.G.BROWN 80-13=67 | 2003 | |
| 1969 | A.A.WATSON 90-20=70* | 2004 | |
| 1970 | T.J.PLUMLEY 83-16=67 | 2005 | |
| 1971 | G.A.REDFERN 80-15=67* | 2006 | |
| 1972 | H.G.BROWN 75-9=66 | 2007 | |

*Brian Meadows, Frank Wild Cup 1975 and President's Finalist 1996, with close friend and long term partner Alan Panter.*

| | |
|---|---|
| 1973  D.WITTS 80-18=72 | 2008 |
| 1974  C.H.HOWKINS 78-13=65 | 2009 |
| 1975  B.MEADOWS 78-18=60 | 2010 |
| 1976  M.D.DANIELS 85-20=65 | 2011 |
| 1977  P.OAKENFULL 79-15=64 | 2012 |
| 1978  L.A.JAMES 81-14=67 | |

* Play Offs
1955 L.Gardiner Runner Up
1964 B.People Runner Up
1965 F.Masson Runner Up
1969 R.Buchan Runner Up
1971 D.McGillivray Runner Up
1979 A.Panter Runner Up
1980 T.Ludlow & P.Braithwaite Runners Up
1983 W.Balshaw & R.J.Frost Runners Up
1984 M.J.Butler & W.H.Sammons Runners Up

# CHAPTER 10

# Dawland Cup

"Integrity is the person you are when nobody is looking"

Methodist Church, Savannah South Carolina April 2001.

**THIS is one of the oldest trophies played for at the Club. It was presented to the Club by Norman Dawson (Captain 1895) and John Haviland (The Club's first Captain 1894). The name Dawland combines the names of the two donors. The trophy is now presented to the winner of the eighteen-hole bogey competition played on the Saturday of the autumn meeting. In earlier times it was played for under medal conditions.**

Tommy (The Mighty) Flynn recorded his only trophy victory in that very hot summer of 1976 when he played some of his best golf holing a "few" putts and lifted the cup in a play off against Alan Parker. He recalls the victory with great passion and wishes that his current handicap of twenty-five could return to its former glory of ten.

Bobby Bason became the last person to win a cup at Kettering Road when he defeated John Haddon in a play-off, the day prior to the course closing on the 5 October 1990. The pair had originally scored a remarkable five up against par. John (Snack) Haddon had sat in the clubhouse for three hours confident that his score was the winning score until Bobby, who was in the last group on the course came in. Snack was so confident that he had the winning score, he had already bought a round of drinks for the all those members in the club! Don't count your chickens before they are hatched. For the record John had in fact won the trophy on two occasions in 1982&7.

Low men have dominated the trophy apart from interventions in 1978, 1993 and 1995 by Les Necus, Ian Griffiths and Ted Marris. Des Southey being the only player to have retained the cup in 1972/3. In 1991 it was won by "the man mountain" Neil Frost with a remarkable score of seven up. Ian Griffiths who scored eight up in 1993 beat this record score.

Bob Knight became the Millenium winner to register his first ever victory and finally lived up to his nickname of "The White Knight" He was ably assisted by caddie John Churchman and they really celebrated at Trophies night. The pair went on to become the Tartan Trophy winners the following year, where their fine play prevented Dean Roberts and Jason Osborne completing the Club's fourball and foursomes double.

*John Haddon 'Big drink for a big man' at Kettering Road 1989.*

| | |
|---|---|
| 1896 | AURTHUR F.FORSTER |
| 1897 | D.ELDER WALKER Nett 82 |
| 1899 | FRED K BOSTOCK |
| 1900 | CHARLES W.PHIPPS 100-16=84 |
| 1901 | FRANK HILL # 94-10=84 |
| 1902 | H.H.OSMOND COOKSON |
| 1903 | D.P.TAYLOR 95-12=83 |
| 1904 | ERIC N.BOSTOCK 91-16=75 |
| 1905 | E.ROGERS BULL 90-9=81 |
| 1906 | V.J.LEATHERDALE 96-10=86 |
| 1907 | R.GRAHAM DAWSON 101-16=85 |
| 1908 | H.CROPLEY |

| | |
|---|---|
| 1959 | D.W.GARLICK +2* |
| 1960 | A.F.STEVENS +2 |
| 1961 | R.G.HALLIDAY +3 |
| 1962 | E.C.KOTTLER +1 |
| 1963 | L.A.JOHNSON +2* |
| 1964 | B.J.AGER +3 |
| 1965 | T.WARING −3 |
| 1966 | J.HALLIWELL all sqr |
| 1967 | J.D.HAWKINS −1* |
| 1968 | T.THOMPSON all sqr |
| 1969 | J.SKELTON +2 |
| 1970 | C.DURANT +5 |

| | | | | |
|---|---|---|---|---|
| 1909 | H.S.SNELL 87-8=79 | | 1971 | R.NEWMAN +5* |
| 1910 | C.W.STRINGER 94-12=82 | | 1972 | D.C.SOUTHEY +2 |
| 1911 | J.KELLETT 90-12=78 | | 1973 | D.C.SOUTHEY +" |
| 1912 | J.H.C.DAWES 93-12=81* | | 1974 | A.F.STEVENS +1 |
| 1913 | G.E.HOLMES 98-12=86 | | 1975 | F.MOSES +5 |
| 1914 | C.WRIGHT 86-12=74 | | 1976 | T.FLYNN +1* |
| WORLD WAR 1 | | | 1977 | A.J.PARKER+2 |
| 1919 | W.H.J.BUNTING 86-6=80 | | 1978 | L.NECUS all sqr |
| 1920 | B.L.CHURCH 91-16=75 | | 1979 | B.J.MEADOWS +1 |
| 1921 | C.WRIGHT 85-7=78 | | 1980 | K.BILLINGHAM +2 |
| 1922 | F.C.WILD 88-24=74 | | 1981 | A.DONALDSON all sqr |
| 1923 | D.DEMPSTER 84-12=72 | | 1982 | J.T.HADDON +1* |
| 1924 | D.DEMPSTER 83-7=76 | | 1983 | A.J.PARKER +1* |
| 1925 | C.G.G.SOUTAR 79-9=70 | | 1984 | K.J.COLES +4 |
| 1926 | G.B.MUSCOTT 91-15=76* | | 1985 | H.McROBERTS +2* |
| 1927 | J.G.TEBBUTT =76 | | 1986 | J.GILLIGAN +2 |
| 1928 | P.HUTTON 87-14=73* | | 1987 | J.T.HADDON +1 |
| 1929 | L.M.CROCKETT 83-12=71 | | 1988 | A.LANE +2* |
| 1930 | P.HUTTON 84-12=72 | | 1989 | A.J.CARTER |
| 1931 | J.H.C.DAWES 86-12=74* | | 1990 | R.W.BASON |
| 1932 | GEO N.SOMERS 76-4=72 | | 1991 | N.J.FROST +7 |
| 1933 | F.G.MANNING 83-16=67 | | 1992 | A.J.PEACOCK |
| 1934 | G.W.MINNEY74-5=69 | | 1993 | I.J.GRIFFITHS +8 |
| 1935 | F.C.ROE 74-0=74* | | 1994 | G.J.RIDDALL |
| 1936 | N.H.ABBOTT 79-11=68 | | 1995 | E.W.MARRIS |
| 1937 | H.P.PASSMORE 72-2=70 | | 1996 | G.J.ANDERSON |
| 1938 | O.J.WHITING 87-17=70 | | 1997 | M.J.POUND |
| 1939 | S.J.MORTON 89-17=72 | | 1998 | R.LEACH |
| 1940 | R.C.COOPER 88-17=71 | | 1999 | G.CONDON* +2 |
| 1941-5 | WORLD WAR 2 | | 2000 | R.W.KNIGHT +4 |
| 1946 | F.G.WATTS +6* | | 2001 | J.PENNINGTON +4 |
| 1947 | W.HOLLINGSWORTH 81-16=75 | | 2002 | |
| 1948 | W.T.SWANNELL | | 2003 | |
| 1949 | A.J.SAUNDERSON | | 2004 | |
| 1950 | F.SHARMAN | | 2005 | |
| 1951 | V.HEARNE | | 2006 | |
| 1952 | S.J.MORTON | | 2007 | |
| 1953 | E.P.JENNINGS | | 2008 | |
| 1954 | F.SKETCHLEY 86-18=68 | | 2009 | |
| 1955 | B.COOKSLEY +1 | | 2010 | |
| 1956 | D.C.SOUTHEY −2 | | 2011 | |
| 1957 | A.LYON +3 | | 2012 | |
| 1958 | A.J.CLARKE -1 | | | |

# Record book says A.E.Phipps
*Play Offs
1912 A.P.Price Runner Up
1926 E.Gavine RU
1928 F.F.Ironside RU
1931 H.W.Clark RU
1935 J.Williamson RU
1946 S.Lovell RU
1959 G.W.Garlick & W.H.Chapman RUs
1963 R.S.Botwood RU
1967 S.Teckman & J.Halliwell RUs
1971 S.Pragnell RU
1975 A.Parker RU
1982 M.Peacock RU
1983 K.V.Morris RU
1985 G.Finedon RU
1988 B.Frost RU
1999 M.J.Izzard & G.Lott RUs
2001 M.M.Woods,
     A.M.Hughes,
     F.Bustin RUs

*Bob Knight, Dawland Cup 2000
and John Churchman, Tartan
Trophy winners 2001.*

# CHAPTER 11

# Stanhope Cup

"I never knew so much that I can't learn more"

Harvey Penick

**MR LOUIS STANHOPE presented the cup on the 15th June 1927 to be awarded on the result of a thirty six-hole medal competition during the autumn meeting. The competition originally was limited to players with a handicap of twenty or less.**

Conrad Ceislewicz in a memorable season picked up the trophy when he reduced his handicap to scratch at the age of fifteen. His father Joseph was very committed to Conrad's development as a golfer and a young man and I often detected his passion when playing with him. Conrad was of the class of Sandy Lyle and Ian Woosnam at British Boys level amongst others and was a real boy's hero to the younger players. His powerful yet graceful swing was the envy of all the young lads. Only schoolmate Chris Westall appeared to be able to touch him from a distance. Weston Favell Secondary Modern School was justifiably very proud of their local achievements. I found these two boys to be inspirational as a fourteen-year-old at the rival local school Cherry Orchard. We used to joke in the changing rooms prior to Rugby matches against gorillas from e.g. Spencer and Corby schools that they were only that good at golf since they did not play Rugby at that Weston Favell school and only played the "poofs game" of Football!

Long standing Club member Len James who for many years owned a hardware shop on Broadmead Avenue became the winner on a very wet day in 1970 with scores of nett 65 and 76. The weather was so bad that day, that many members did not complete thirty-six holes, since the waterproofs available then simply could not cope with the very strong rain. This was Len's first trophy at the Club, which he subsequently added to in 1978 when he won the Spencer and Frank Wild Cups. Len knew my father Les as a school chum, since they both attended Kettering Road Junior School. One could say therefore that I have been loosely associated with the club since the 1930's. Len is now in his eightieth year and looks very well on it too. His passion for sport is still present and he was recently up at the Club in a packed spike bar to watch England's football team successfully defeat Greece in the World Cup qualifier. The long serving and passionate Hollingsworth and Scratch League captain Gary Addington has won the trophy twice in 1983&95.

Young gun Alex Izzard retained the trophy for his family in 2000 when he emulated the author's win in 1999. Alex's victory included a fast start in the morning round where he was four under par after eight holes, just like the old man the previous year.

Many players' say emulated although the wiser one's respectfully suggests that he is taking over the mantle!

At the Kettering Road course players from handicaps of scratch to eighteen won the trophy whereas at Harlestone low handicappers have dominated it. In 2001 Dominic Jessup completed the hat-trick of 36 hole medal competitions, when he added this trophy to his 1993 Club Championship and the 1999 Soutar Cup victories. With these fine rounds Dominic's handicap reached scratch for the first time in his life, offering the potential to play on the Senior's circuit in due course with his relative Mike Lynch.

| | | | |
|---|---|---|---|
| 1927 | F.M.JONES 188-40=148 | 1970 | L.A.JAMES 64+77=141 |
| 1928 | J.DUNLOP 153-10=143 | 1971 | T.WAREING 66+71=137 |
| 1929 | G.MARKIE Nett 55 | 1972 | K.W.ROEBUCK 71+70=141 |
| 1930 | G.CROFT Nett 50 | 1973 | J.M.PETTIGREW 67+64=131 |
| 1931 | P.G.JONES 168-18=150 | 1974 | H.R.BEIRNE 74+68=142 |
| 1932 | F.GARRARD 181-28=153 | 1975 | M.J.BUTLER 65+67=132 |
| 1933 | S.RICHARDS 146 | 1976 | D.GEE 67+71=138* |
| 1934 | P.G.JONES 148 | 1977 | M.PARRY 69+72=141 |
| 1935 | C.LAW 69+73=142 | 1978 | E.POTTER 72+70=142 |
| 1936 | A.McFARLAND 175-38=137 | 1979 | M.M.WOODS 65+72=132 |
| 1937 | R.S.JELLEYMAN 65+70=135 | 1980 | A.G.WEST 71+67=138 |
| 1938 | F.ALIBONE 71+73=144 | 1981 | R.M.PAGE 69+63=132 |
| 1939 | L.G.HASDELL 172-28+144 | 1982 | P.B.COULSON 65+67=132 |
| 1940 | W.C.REYNOLDS 176-38+138 | 1983 | G.P.ADDINGTON 70+64=134* |
| 1941 | E.FULLER 183-30=143 | 1984 | A.J.PEACOCK 63+69=132 |
| 1942 | L.G.HASDELL 172-24=148 | 1985 | G.J.RIDDALL 62+65=127 |
| 1943 | R.W.HALLIWELL 89-20=69 | 1986 | D.C.PRIOR 67+68=135 |
| 1944 | W.CRESSWELL 74+64=138 | 1987 | P.STONES 68+71=139 |
| 1945 | G.H.WILD 73+69=142 | 1988 | J.T.HADDON 64+66=130 |
| 1946 | R.E.GUBBINS 169-30=139 | 1989 | A.DONALDSON |

*Tom Kelly, Stanhope Cup winner 1993, with Club Captain Geoff Garbutt.*

| | | | |
|---|---|---|---|
| 1947 | S.R.LOVELL | 1990 | R.T.F.WILLOUGHBY |
| 1948 | A.J.HARRISON | 1991 | P.HIRST 68+69=137* |
| 1949 | D.F.FISHER | 1992 | A.S.BOND |
| 1950 | P.RUSHTON | 1993 | T.KELLY 72+63=135 |
| 1951 | P.J.GAINSFORD | 1994 | G.H.SLINN 69+69=138 |
| 1952 | J.W.TAYLOR | 1995 | G.P.ADDINGTON 71+69 |
| 1953 | R.W.CLARKE | 1996 | S.EBORALL 67+74=141* |
| 1954 | R.L.CLARKE 71+71=142 | 1997 | A.J.CARTER |
| 1955 | M.R.CLARKE 75+74=149 | 1998 | G.CONDON |
| 1956 | F.A.THORNTON 66+72=138 | 1999 | M.J.IZZARD 140-10=130 |
| 1957 | R.G.HALLIDAY 66+68=134 | 2000 | A.J.IZZARD 148-8=140 |
| 1958 | R.G.RIDDICK 74+76=150 | 2001 | D.J.JESSUP 139-2=137 |
| 1959 | C.J.BRYDON 73+64+137 | 2002 | |
| 1960 | M.S.FLOYD 68+69=137 | 2003 | |
| 1961 | P.E.StQUINTON 66+62=128 | 2004 | |
| 1962 | F.W.THORPE 69+69=138 | 2005 | |
| 1963 | F.V.SMART 65+73=142 | 2006 | |
| 1964 | R.M.BUCHAN 75+66=141 | 2007 | |
| 1965 | W.PETTIGREW 70+75=145 | 2008 | |
| 1966 | D.SPRUCE 67+71=138 | 2009 | |
| 1967 | E.H.WHITTAKER 67+69=138 | 2010 | |
| 1968 | J.M.PETTIGREW 74+75=149 | 2011 | |
| 1969 | C.R.CIESLEWICZ 71+68=139 | 2012 | |

*Play Offs
1976 M.Haddon Runner Up
1983 P.McKenzie RU
1991 M.Peacock RU
1996 J.Smith RU

# CHAPTER 12

# Northampton Cup

"If I could take out of my life everything but my experiences in St Andrews I would still have had a rich, full life"

Robert Tyre "Bobby" Jones, co-inventor of The Masters Tournament at his Freedom of the City presentation 9 Oct 1958.

**PRIOR to the Nett competition which we know as The Northampton Cup, the Club held a 36 hole open scratch competition which was first played for in 1895 and won by A.J.Robertson from Tooting. In 1895 the competition was called the Northampton Challenge Bowl open to amateurs for 36 holes medal play over the Northampton "links" It attracted players from local Clubs and from far and wider places such as Cheltenham, Formby and Hunstanton. A field of thirty or so players was typical at that time. The competition became a nett trophy in 1902. In the first ten years that it was played for, two players A.J.Robertson and D.C.Scroggie notched up a hat trick of victories each.**

Presented by the Club committee on the 20th May 1927 the beautiful rose bowl trophy was originally competed for by the various winners of the medal and bogey competitions held alternatively over 36 holes medal as a nett competition. It is also one of the oldest competitions played for at the Club, along with the Spencer Cup.

In modern times since the late sixties, eight qualifying rounds are now played for in three handicap divisions producing a twenty four man final which is played over thirty six holes in September. The handicap divisions are scratch to twelve, thirteen to eighteen and nineteen to twenty eight. This is one of the most desirable trophies to win due to the historic associations with Club; the difficulty of initially qualifying and also since the final is played over thirty-six holes of medal golf.

*Gary Slinn, Northampton Cup winner and Nett League Champion 1995.*

Since those early days of the club, only Tony Stevens in the 1960's has managed to win the trophy three times, which were in fact three victories in four years. In the focus of this book the trophy has been won by low and high handicappers, young and old players. Chris Westall being the only golfer to have won the cup twice at the tender ages of fifteen in 1969 and eighteen in 1972 respectively. Dennis "the tomahawk" Pritchard collected the trophy in 1970 where he managed to keep his fiery temperament under control and maintained the right level of aggression versus relaxation. Keith Vallance, who played cricket to a high level locally, added this to his impressive list of trophy wins in 1971 with an excellent score of 71+66. Keith was playing in first game on the course and was able to set his own rapid pace on the 19 September. His winning were the trophy, a momento, a voucher and £2-90p in the sweep! I was very fortunate to collect the trophy in 1979 despite almost not go out for the second eighteen holes. My first round was so bad I thought that I had no chance of winning. If Kevin Newman had not persuaded me to go out with himself and Norman Jones the story would have been totally different. A salutary lesson to someone as immature as I was, at that time.

The 1982 Winner should have been Alan Linney, who scored 69 gross in the morning round, to be six shots clear of the field. He did not win the trophy since he had agreed to attend the author's wedding in the afternoon! A great friendly gesture symptomatic of the man.

There was some "friendly controversy around the table" at Trophies night over the 1985 winner, John Higginbottom. Having been presented with the trophy everyone remarked upon what a good score he had returned. As a casual remark around the dinner table John said " O yes the only hole I had trouble with was the eighth, where I had to hit my ball over the dry stone wall in to the farmyard." At this point many an eyebrow was raised since the ball was technically out of bounds. There was a rapid exchange of views on rules concerning what to do, could one do anything? With John's memory one could not be certain that what he thought he had remembered may not have actually taken place. In the end sleeping dogs were allowed to lie. He was a lovely man, who had a gentle demeanour despite all the suffering he had gone through in the previous two years. He was so happy to have won and enjoyed filling the trophy with a suitable beverage for all to consume. The 1988 winner was Mark Britten who captured the trophy in a remarkable season where he also won the Club Championship and the Coronation Cup. Mark was a very good medal player though a poor match player and never qualified for the Match play final. Mark is no longer a member of the Club having gone his own way, he was a slightly lonely character who had become the villain in the 1987 Hollingsworth semi-final at Wellingborough. The "Brain" story is described in detail in the Centenary book starting on page 144. The story described him hitting a driver on the eighteenth at Wellingborough, one of the tightest and most demanding holes in the County. The choice of club being totally incorrect especially when we were one up and teed off second. Dominic Jessup has still not forgiven him!

I suspect that the proudest winner to date was Rob Willoughby in 1989 who returned a bandit like score of 60 + 66 nett over the Kettering road course to record his first trophy victory with the lowest score ever recorded in this competition. His handicap came down significantly that day! Through the nineties the trophy was split between medium handicap winners of Bob Carter, Graham Castle, Alan Pardoe, Gary Slinn, Danny West and Ian Hemsley together with a few low men. These include Gavin Riddall (67+70 nett), David Dare (64+72) nett and Andy Carter (can't remember + can't remember nett!)

Gary Slinn's victory in 1995 was notable as it completed what he describes as " The Nett League and Cup Double" since he had already secured the Nett League Championship "by a country mile"

The Millenium winner was Simon Freshwater who scored a remarkable 63+72 nett off a ten handicap. His morning round of one over par opened up a huge lead where no one was able to catch him. This round included a six at the fourth hole, where his tee shot rebounded of the stone wall on the edge of the woods and finished out of bounds behind him! When shown the trophy he had just won, he simply could not believe how beautiful it was, and that he had just become part of the history of Northampton Golf Club.

*Young Richard Lovelady tees off from the second tee in winter at Kettering Road.*

| | | | | |
|---|---|---|---|---|
| 1895 | A.J.ROBERTSON | | 1962 | A.F.STEVENS 66-71=137 |
| 1896 | AURTHUR.F.FORSTER 187 | | 1963 | A.F.STEVENS 73-69=142 |
| | | | | (7scores returned) |
| 1897 | A.J.ROBERTSON 79-88=162 | | 1964 | J.M.PETTIGREW 73-72=145 |
| 1898 | R.H.FERGUSON | | 1965 | M.EVERITT |
| 1899 | R.H.FERGUSON | | 1966 | B.W.SCOTT |
| 1900 | D.C.SCROGGIE 100-88=188 | | 1967 | J.T.CIESLEWICZ |
| 1901 | A.J.ROBERTSON 93-90=183 | | 1968 | C.J.TURNER 72-72 |
| 1902 | H.H.OSMOND COOKSON | | | |
| | 181-16=165 | | 1969 | C.S.WESTALL 67-68=135 |
| 1903 | D.C.SCROGGIE | | | |
| | 87gross-87=174Nett | | 1970 | J.D.PRITCHARD 72-68=140 |
| 1904 | D.C.SCROGGIE | | 1971 | K.J.VALLANCE 71-66=137 |
| 1905 | A.ANDERSON 78-83=163 | | 1972 | C.S.WESTALL 69-73=142 |
| 1906 | EDWARD.E.EDDOWES | | | |
| | 74-79=153 | | 1973 | D.McGILLIVRAY 67-74=141 |
| 1907 | H.CROPLEY 82-84=166 | | 1974 | T.J.LUDLOW 73-70=143 |
| 1908 | HERBERT MOBBS 72-78=150 | | 1975 | K.NEWMAN 75-64=139 |
| 1909 | A.J.FRASER 79-87=166 | | 1976 | R.SWANN 67-66=133 |
| 1910 | J.KELLETT 80-81=161 | | 1977 | F.A.JOHNSON 70-69+139* |
| 1911 | EDGAR.I.VOKES 87-82=169 | | 1978 | T.K.JAMES 169-30=139 |
| 1912 | G.A.T.VIALS 78-82=160 | | 1979 | M.J.IZZARD 151-10=141 |
| 1913 | G.P.M.SKAE 73-77=150 | | 1980 | D.S.CAMERON 159-16 |
| 1928 | A.J.ALIBONE 139 | | 1981 | R.SWIFT 163-28=135 |
| 1929 | J.DUNLOP | | 1982 | I.SMITH 160-24=136 |
| 1930 | F.ALIBONE 162-14=148 | | 1983 | R.PALMER 165-24=141 |
| 1931 | D.F.JOHNSTONE 164-22=142 | | 1984 | W.RAGBIR 174-36=138 |
| 1932 | F.ALIBONE 159-16=143 | | 1985 | J.HIGGINBOTTOM |
| | | | | 183-54=129 |
| 1933 | N.W.BRABNER | | 1986 | C.MacKENZIE 67-67=134 |
| 1934 | I.M.ALLISON 146 | | 1987 | K.BROWNLESS 70-67=137 |
| 1935 | R.S.JELLEYMAN 159-16=143 | | 1988 | M.BRITTEN 65-67=137 |
| 1936 | J.DAVIDSON | | 1989 | R.WILLOUGHBY 60-66=126 |
| 1937 | C.S.CATLOW 141-0=141 | | 1990 | J.WILLSHER |
| 1938 | J.I.H.MEIER 72-76=148 | | 1991 | R.R.CARTER 63-68=141 |
| 1939 | S.N.HILL 182-34=148 | | 1992 | G.D.CASTLE 71-72=143 |
| 1940 | J.E.GIFFIN 169-22=147 | | 1993 | A.A.PARDOE |
| 1941 | A.L.WARD 167-2=156? | | 1994 | G.J.RIDDALL 67-70=137 |
| 1942 | A.S.ALIBONE 156-6=150 | | 1995 | G.H.SLINN 71-70=141 |
| 1943 | A.J.FAULKNER 182-34=148 | | 1996 | I.HEMSLEY |
| 1944 | W.H.KNIGHT 184-44=140 | | 1997 | D.A.DARE 64-72=136* |
| 1945 | W.CRESSWELL151-8=143 | | 1998 | D.WEST |
| 1946 | A.E.TEESDALE 191-48=143 | | 1999 | A.J.CARTER |
| 1947 | E.COKER 80-7=73 | | 2000 | S.FRESHWATER 63-72=135 |
| 1948 | M.DUNKLEY | | 2001 | D.GORE 73-71=144 |

| | |
|---|---|
| 1949 D.F.FISHER | 2002 |
| 1950 R.L.CLARKE | 2003 |
| 1951 T.HULL | 2004 |
| 1952 M.R.CLARKE | 2005 |
| 1953 R.C.ANDERSON | 2006 |
| 1954 R.S.MUMFORD | 2007 |
| 1955 E.G.HARLEY | 2008 |
| 1956 D.G.ROBERTS | 2009 |
| 1957 H.OLLERTON | 2010 |
| 1958 A.J.CLARKE 70-69=139 | 2011 |
| 1959 P.E.StQUINTON | 2012 |
| 1960 A.F.STEVENS 73-67 (8 played) | 2013 |
| 1961 I.H.CUTHBERT 66-66=132 | 2014 |

*Play Offs
1938 A.J.Faulkner RU
1941 L.G.Hasdell RU
1977 K.Billingham & L.Russell RUs
1984 T.Addington RU
1997 G.J.Riddall & Mr. Thompson RUs

# CHAPTER 13

# Summer Knockout

"Victory is always sweet. But to win at St Andrews is so special it rises above everything else"

Seve Ballesteros Open Champion 1984

**THE trophy was bought by the Club from Club funds and is awarded to the winner of a knockout competition played during the summer. The top thirty-two players from an eighteen hole qualifier competing. The final is competed over thirty-six holes.**

This trophy has been dominated by the low handicappers over the last thirty years. Twice Jim Pettigrew, David Dare, Dominic Jessup and yours truly have won it. Only Paul Humphris, Ted Jagger, Mike Pepper and Mike Blake "interrupting" the low handicap flow. The trophy suits the low men despite the amount of run that there is on the ball in the summer months which one might imagine could help the longer handicap players. It will be interesting to see whether the change from three quarters of the handicap difference to full difference affects who wins the trophy. The organising bodies i.e. The English Golf Union claim that this move will not affect the percentage of low handicappers that will win singles competitions but it will make the winning margins smaller. It is fair to say that most people are not yet convinced by this hypothesis. This change appears to fly in the face of the long held belief that the object of play was to try and reduce ones handicap whenever possible and to strive to get as low a handicap as possible. Only time will tell.

Martin Harris became a worthy winner of the Millennium competition, however there is a Steward's Enquiry concerning the composition of the tobacco found in his pipe. He may be asked to take a dope test, his wife Sue recently stated that she is absolutely certain he would be able to pass it! This was Martin's fourth trophy victory in a long and successful

*St. Andrews, 'The Home of Golf'.*

association with the club, his first victory coming in 1979 in the Coronation Cup. He is, along with Gavin Condon, one of only two players to have won both the Summer and Winter knockout competitions.

The two trophies, have only been won once in the same year by the great player Charles Catlow in 1936. Charles was perhaps the County's finest player to date and became County Champion a staggering eleven times, his modest son, Richard, becoming the County's first Honorary Life Member, also having made a major contribution to County Golf.

The 2001 final was Dean Robert's third 36 holes final of the year, I think he has worn out the caddie by now. He narrowly lost to Adrian Peacock in a sporting final. Dean was in fact three up at lunch, Adrian getting back to all square on the twelve before securing victory on the seventeenth with a level par score. This match was played in front of the 2001 Match Play final where Adrian's lodger, Simon Tootell was victorious. I rather suspect the house celebrated that evening in style!

| | |
|---|---|
| 1924 C.G.G.SOUTAR | 1972 J.M.PETTIGREW |
| 1925 J.H.C.DAWES | 1973 J.M.PETTIGREW |
| 1926 L.M.DAVIES | 1974 M.J.IZZARD |
| 1927 O.J.HARGRAVE | 1975 M.J.IZZARD |
| 1928 J.DUNLOP | 1976 J.A.COSTIN |
| 1929 L.W.WILD | 1977 D.A.DARE |
| 1930 F.C.ROE | 1978 K.BILLINGHAM |
| 1931 R.JUSTICE | 1979 P.A.HUMPHRIS |
| 1932 D.F.JOHNSTONE | 1980 R.M.PAGE |
| 1933 G.W.MINNEY | 1981 K.J.COLES |
| 1934 A.S.ALIBONE | 1982 E.JAGGER |
| 1935 C.S.CATLOW | 1983 R.J.C.KILLIP |
| 1936 C.S.CATLOW | 1984 D.A.DARE |
| 1937 A.S.ALIBONE | 1985 K.BILLINGHAM |
| 1938 F.C.ROE | 1986 K.BROWNLESS |
| 1939 W.K.S.SMITH | 1987 A.J.CARTER |
| 1940-45 World War2 | 1988 D.J.JESSUP |
| 1945 J.B.CORRIN | 1989 G.J.RIDDALL |
| 1946 J.E.GIFFIN | 1990 C.CONNOLLY |
| 1947 S.J.MORTON | 1991 J.SHEPHERD |
| 1948 A.J.HARRISON | 1992 P.J.SMITH |
| 1949 B.A.MARBROOK | 1993 M.W.PEPPER |
| 1950 J.W.TAYLOR | 1994 D.J.JESSUP |
| 1951 J.W.TAYLOR | 1995 M.J.BLAKE |
| 1952 R.S.MUMFORD | 1996 J.OSBORNE |
| 1953 R.C.ANDERSON | 1997 A.J.PEACOCK |
| 1954 R.J.PATERSON | 1998 G.CONDON |
| 1955 D.C.SOUTHEY | 1999 M.J.POUND |
| 1956 A.ANDERSON | 2000 M.R.HARRIS |
| 1957 N.JONES | 2001 A.J.PEACOCK 2/1 |
| 1958 N.JONES | 2002 |
| 1959 J.A.EYTON-JONES | 2003 |
| 1960 R.BIERNE | 2004 |
| 1961 B.N.JONES | 2005 |
| 1962 R.G.AITKEN | 2006 |
| 1963 P.ST.QUINTON | 2007 |
| 1964 G.D.COLES | 2008 |
| 1965 T.WARING | 2009 |
| 1966 A.F.STEVENS | 2010 |
| 1967 J.D.PRITCHARD | 2011 |
| 1968 R.A.FLOWERS | 2012 |
| 1969 H.BUCKENHAM | 2013 |
| 1970 A.F.STEVENS | 2014 |
| 1971 M.P.RUDKIN | 2015 |

*Richard Lovelady pitches to the seventh green at Kettering Road,
or has he shanked it?*

# CHAPTER 14

# President's Trophies

"Golf is twenty per cent mechanics and technique. The other eighty per cent is philosophy, humour, tragedy, romance, melodrama, companionship, cussedness and conversation"

Grantland Rice

**THE pair of trophies was presented by W. (Bill) Hollingsworth to commemorate his becoming President in 1964 to be competed for as a fourball betterball knockout during the summer months.**

At that time many golfers played each other on a Sunday morning at Kettering Road where play always started at eight o clock from the first, third, fifth, seventh, eighth, tenth, thirteenth and sixteenth tee. This format ensured that everyone completed their round at the same time and could be in the clubhouse together to hear the Captain's speech at one o clock. The format has changed now slightly to include a thirty six-hole final. In the time honoured fashion the trophy is presented by the Club's President on trophies night. These trophies are much sought after by the players and one cannot praise highly enough President Bill Hollingsworth (1964-1982) enough for his vision. One of my great memories of the old Club was seeing President (1982-1990) Harold Shenfield proudly presenting the trophies surrounded by cigar smoke. President John Eyton Jones (1990-1991) was a great supporter of local golf and loved his golf, especially if he was playing in a friendly fourball for nett birdies! Sadly these distinguished gentlemen are no longer physically with us.

In its first year the trophies were won fittingly by past County President Tony Stevens and the current Club President Thomas Charles Austin Knight. The trophies have been won three time by brothers in the form of Charles and John Rouse in 1967, Bill and Richard Botwood in 1970 and John and Ron Halliwell in 1975.

*Geoff Hanson and Mike Spicer, President's Trophy winners 1989.*

*Trophies Night celebrations 1989 at Kettering Road.*

In 1980 Kevin Newman was playing some of the best golf of his life and won the trophies with Mike Shelford. This completed a superb year for Kevin when he was also a member of the winning Anglian League B Team and the Old Northamptonian team, which won the Chronicle and Echo foursomes trophy at Kingsthorpe.

The 1983 semi-final between the author partnered by Dennis Tyrell against Holland and Coulson was notable since Derek did not speak for the whole round. Del boy Holland eventual holing a ten foot par putt to ensure victory on the eighteenth where he simply said "A pleasure". Almost predictably, they went on to win the final in style for Derek's first and only entry on the Clubs honours boards. I was again involved in the final stages of the 1984 event against Charles Durant and Derek Hodder and once again lost on the last putt on the last green. This was despite back to back eagle threes on the par five fifth and sixth holes where Charles in his gentlemanly way stated "I think you are trying to win this." Once again they went on to win the trophies. My partner's shanked eight iron in front of the bunker on the eighteenth is implanted in my memory and will haunt us both forever. I shall not mention the name of the gentlemen, my long-term friend who I used to pass the rugby ball to at Cherry Orchard School.

The 1989 final witnessed an amazing come back from Hanson and Spicer who were eight down with sixteen holes to play and won on the last against G.P.Addington and J.Moorcroft. Young Gary Addington has played the first eighteen holes in level par to go into lunch six up. I was playing the eighteenth hole that day and as I passed them on the third tee, their twenty first hole I half seriously remarked "See you in about an hour", having established the current score. As the members sat in the clubhouse and waited and waited we had no idea what was transpiring. Eventually the fourball came down the last hole; the eerie atmosphere was detectable from a long distance. They all looked completely drained and as though they had been in a war! Both pairs actually had putts for victory before Mike Spicer and Geoff Hanson eventually won this marathon match.

The 1990 competition was notable, since the eventual winners played all their early rounds at Kettering Road prior to the 36 hole final at Harlestone in October. Richard Palmer and Richard Pugh eventually winning by one up. In recent finals (1994,1998 and 2000) scores of some matches have been as high as victory by nine and eight and a concession on the twenty third hole.

Bob Willoughby and Peter Beeby won the trophies in 1993 having disposed of the author and partner in the semi-final to complete for me a hat trick of losses to the eventual winners. I began to wonder if I might ever get my hands on this treasured trophy.

Bob and Peter defeated close friends Phil Smith and Kevin Coles in the final. Phil and Kevin eventually winning the trophy in 1995 despite Phil hitting the old tree to the right of the tenth tee in every round!

Three other golfers together with the author have featured twice on the trophy. Keith Vallance's silky swing with a hint of the off-drive bringing victory in 1968 and twenty years later in 1988. Phil Smith also became victorious with different partners in 1995 and 2000. Glenn Keates and partner during a vintage season for them became the first pair ever to win the trophies on two occasions in 1996 and 1998. The final in 1998 was notable since runner up Martin Harris holed his tee shot on the twentieth hole using a four iron which literally pitched in the hole. His partner Ian Farmer still cannot believe how a slightly drawn iron can stay in the hole, we all heard the "clank" of ball hitting flag which must have completely absorbed the pace of the tee shot. Following a long illness, which kept him away from the club for over a year, we were all very pleased to see President Tom Knight at the 1998 trophies night where he proudly presented the trophies.

No pair has to date managed to retain the trophies, which is not too surprising since the format of the competition, fourball betterball off handicap always seems to produce shock results. For example the author and playing partner Glenn Keates were seven under par gross after sixteen holes in the first round of the 2001 tournament and still lost 4/2 to Paul and Darren Mattacola! In 2001 Dean Roberts and Jason Osborne discarded their disappointments from the Hollingsworth trophy to become worthy winners in a closely fought final by 2&1, they were never behind against Steve Tyrell and Alan Broadbent.

*Robert Baker and Neville Kny, President's Trophy winners 1987 with Club President Harold Shenfield.*

| | | | | |
|---|---|---|---|---|
| 1964 | A.F.STEVENS<br>T.C.A.KNIGHT 6/5 | | 1988 | K.J.VALLANCE<br>A.WEST |
| 1965 | W.FLYNN<br>R.STEVENS | | 1989 | G.E.HANSON<br>M.F.A.SPICER 1up |
| 1966 | D.MONTGOMERY<br>R.MATTHWEWS | | 1990 | R.PALMER<br>S.PUGH |
| 1967 | J.T.ROUSE<br>C.ROUSE | | 1991 | S.J.BAILEY<br>M.BRITTEN |
| 1968 | J.M.PETTIGREW<br>K.J.VALLANCE | | 1992 | A.HARRISON<br>J.SHEPHERD 2/1 |
| 1969 | G.MACE<br>R.EARL | | 1993 | P.L.BEEBY<br>R.T.F.WILLOUGHBY 6/4 |
| 1970 | W.G.BOTWOOD<br>R.I.BOTWOOD | | 1994 | K.HEARD<br>S.EBORALL 8/7 |
| 1971 | W.LORYMAN<br>D.MABBUTT | | 1995 | K.J.COLES<br>P.J.SMITH 4/3 |
| 1972 | J.GILLIGAN<br>G.FAULKNER | | 1996 | M.J.IZZARD<br>G.H.KEATES 4/3 |
| 1973 | D.FORREST<br>T.PEARSON | | 1997 | N.J.FROST<br>C.MacKENZIE 3/2 |
| 1974 | T.J.LUDLOW<br>A.WRIGHT | | 1998 | M.J.IZZARD<br>G.H.KEATES 9/8 |
| 1975 | J.W.HALLIWELL<br>R.W.HALLIWELL | | 1999 | I.A.DAKIN<br>G.D.CASTLE |
| 1976 | C.J.TURNER<br>J.SKELTON | | 2000 | M.J.POUND<br>P.J.SMITH 8 up after 23 C |
| 1977 | J.COSTIN<br>D.MacDONALD | | 2001 | J.OSBORNE<br>D.J.ROBERTS 2&1 |
| 1978 | J.A.SALE<br>N.A.WHITE | | 2002 | |
| 1979 | A.A.WATSON<br>K.GORE | | 2003 | |
| 1980 | K.NEWMAN<br>M.SHELFORD | | 2004 | |
| 1981 | H.E.RICHARD<br>W.A.SHELTON | | 2005 | |
| 1982 | L.JARVIS<br>T.MURFIN | | 2006 | |
| 1983 | D.J.HOLLAND<br>P.B.COULSON | | 2007 | |
| 1984 | C.DURANT<br>D.HODDER | | 2008 | |
| 1985 | D.EVANS<br>D.WHITEHEAD | | 2009 | |

1986  P.M.H.REES                          2010
        G.J.RIDDALL
1987  N.T.KNY                             2011
        R.BAKER

"None of us are as smart as all of us"

Japanese Proverb

*R. T. F. Willoughby and Pete Beeby, President's Trophy winners 1993*
*with the losing finalists and 1995 winners Phil Smith and Kevin Coles.*

# CHAPTER 15

# Tartan Trophy

"The man that invented golf and said it is fun is the same man that invented bag pipes and said it was "music"

Anon

**This trophy was presented by W. (Bill) Pettigrew and C. (Charles) Bryden in 1983 to promote "The Scottish" interest in the Club. The top sixteen pairs from a medal qualifier compete for this foursomes competition. Foursomes is in itself a very difficult game which many golfers do not like. When a player comes off the eighteenth hole there are often two feelings stated a) I only feel like I have played nine holes. b) I physically feel that I have played nine, but I am emotionally drained. Such is the great game of foursomes golf.**

Rumour has it that the foursomes format originated from Scotland since a typical tight Scotsman could be the only person likely to invent a game where he could share a golf ball, preferably one supplied by his partner! This is one of the oldest forms of play.

The inaugural winners were Bob Buswell and Brian Ollive in1983; the subsequent winners have been almost exclusively low handicap golfers. This is not too surprising in view of the difficulty of the foursomes game. This is amplified in the Hollingsworth trophy where year by year the teams in the final are nearly always made up of low handicap players. I guess that overall they tend to make proportionately fewer errors in this style of competition. Albert Carter during the 1985 final at Kettering road holed his shot from under the lip of the cavernous bunker on the right of the ninth hole. This great shot did not in the end alter the final outcome where the father and son combination of Albert and Andy Carter were eventually beaten. Having sacked his father as a partner, Andy went on to become a winner the following year with David Evans. Well-known Club members Dave Eborall and Ben Middleton lifted the trophy in 1993 to record Ben's first male win. Ben is one player who is quite a competitor and is passionate about his performance. This passion sometimes overflows in the form of an "emotional outburst" when the result of the shot is not that expected from the mind. A scenario that I am quite familiar with! Dave Eborall on the other hand is a very relaxed character who appears to not have a care in the world and never seems stressed. They obviously made a good combination.

Millennium winners were Keith Vallance and Brian Page who defeated the fancied combination of Jon Lloyd and Simon Tootell by two and one. This pair has over the years become a tried and tested outfit, their first victory in this competition coming thirteen years ago in 1987. They became only the second pair to have won the trophy twice along with Glenn Keates and partner. Keith together with the author is one of only two players, to have won this trophy and the other men's pair' competition the Presidents trophy twice, in a golfing career from the 1960's to the present time. He accomplished this great feat with three different partners in 1968,1988 (President's Jim Pettigrew & Alan West ) 1987 and 2000 (Tartan-Brian Page).

*Keith Vallance and Brian Page, Tartan Trophy winners 1987, with Captain Roger Starmer.*

| | | | |
|---|---|---|---|
| 1983 | R.G.BUSWELL<br>B.J.OLLIVE | 1998 | M.J.IZZARD<br>G.H.KEATES 10/8 |
| 1984 | J.T.HADDON<br>T.J.LUDLOW | 1999 | A.J.LIMBERT<br>D.J.JESSUP |
| 1985 | M.J.IZZARD<br>A.J.LINNEY 3/2 | 2000 | K.J.VALLANCE<br>R.M.PAGE 3/2 |
| 1986 | A.J.CARTER<br>D.EVANS | 2001 | R.KNIGHT<br>J.CHURCHMAN 4/3 |
| 1987 | K.VALLANCE<br>B.PAGE | 2002 | |
| 1988 | D.J.JESSUP<br>T.J.PANTHER | 2003 | |
| 1989 | A.LANE<br>H.E.RICHARDS 2up | 2004 | |
| 1990 | C.PAINTIN<br>J.HARWOOD | 2005 | |
| 1991 | G.P.ADDINGTON<br>C.MacKENZIE 1up | 2006 | |
| 1992 | M.BRITTEN<br>R.D.HOLDING | 2007 | |
| 1993 | D.E.EBORALL<br>B.A.MIDDLETON 7/6 | 2008 | |
| 1994 | A.J.PEACOCK<br>G.J.RIDDALL 6/5 | 2009 | |
| 1995 | M.J.IZZARD<br>G.H.KEATES 4/2 | 2010 | |
| 1996 | S.J.BAILEY<br>A.J.CARTER | 2011 | |
| 1997 | D.A.DARE<br>J.M.LLOYD 3/1 | 2012 | |

*Two demanding second shots at Harlestone, to the first green (above)
and eighth green below.*

# CHAPTER 16

# Grandfather Putter

".backwards understood be only can but, forwards lived be must Life"

Kierkegaard Soren

THIS trophy was presented by Past Captain David Prior and is played for as an eighteen-hole medal. David in fact became the inaugural winner with a fine score of 63 nett. Rudy Ragbir became Champion in 1992 to finally record his first male trophy win having lost in the final of the Matchplay Championship in 1979 and in the play off for the 1983 Coronation Cup. He has of course been quite successful in the mixed scene. Another past Captain joined David on the winning podium, Ben Middleton in 1997. Senior organiser Jack Bird, at the age of seventy-three recorded a fine score of nett sixty four to become the 1994 winner. The Millenium winner was Alan Findley.

| | | | |
|---|---|---|---|
| 1991 | D.C.PRIOR Nett 63 | 2002 | |
| 1992 | R.RAGBIR | 2003 | |
| 1993 | A.R.MOIR | 2004 | |
| 1994 | J.D.BIRD Nett 64 | 2005 | |
| 1995 | J.CUNNINGHAM | 2006 | |
| 1996 | B.R.CLEMENTS | 2007 | |
| 1997 | B.A.MIDDLETON | 2008 | |
| 1998 | R.G.BUSWELL | 2009 | |
| 1999 | V.E.JONES | 2010 | |
| 2000 | A.FINDLEY 68 | 2011 | |
| 2001 | R.M.SAVAGE 64 | 2012 | |

*Head greenkeeper Bert Prigmore with Dolores and Sarah.*

# CHAPTER 17

# League Championship Gross and Nett

"Competitive golf is played mainly on a five and a half inch course, the space between your ears"

Bobby Jones

THE league championship trophies were initially started in 1984 as the brainchild of David Dare and Ken Billingham who presented the Nett trophy. The medal rounds throughout the year accumulate points, which are awarded to the top twenty scores on a twenty down to one basis. There are fifteen qualifying medals consisting of the Summer Knockout qualifier, eight Northampton cup rounds, the thirty six-hole spring meeting medal (Soutar Cup), the fifty four holes of the autumn meeting (Frank Wild & Stanhope Cups) and the Winter knockout qualifier. The best ten scores from the fifteen medals determined the winner up until 1999, when the format was changed such that the winner was the leading points scorer after the last competition. Since 1999 the competition has been open to all competitors and not restricted to only those players that entered. Appropriately David won the trophy in its first outing. The gross trophy was presented in 1991 by the Club.

The results below speak for themselves, not too surprisingly the good medal players feature very strongly, the inconsistency and creative flair of match players being lost over a season of medal performances. Dominic Jessup, Glenn Keates and Andy Carter have registered four, five and five victories each; from a possible twenty eight starts and completed the double of both trophies. Since 1994 young players with a low handicap have dominated the competitions. There has been a tie only once for the Nett trophy in 1998 between close friends Alex Wray and Gavin Condon.

In 2001 following a rich vein of form, Glenn Keates may well win the Nett trophy playing of a handicap of plus one! During this period of play his handicap briefly reached plus two, which was the first time a player had reached this level in the history of the Club.

| | Gross | Nett |
|------|-------|------|
| 1984 | | D.A.DARE |
| 1985 | | K.J.VALLANCE 131 pts |
| 1986 | | G.J.RIDDALL 141 pts |
| 1987 | | A.J.CARTER 143 pts |
| 1988 | | T.F.JONES 144 pts |
| 1989 | | P.B.COULSON |
| 1990 | | G.J.RIDDALL |
| 1991 | D.J.JESSUP 161pts | D.J.JESSUP |
| 1992 | D.J.JESSUP | D.J.JESSUP |
| 1993 | D.J.JESSUP | J.SHEPHERD |
| 1994 | G.H.KEATES | G.H.KEATES |
| 1995 | G.H.KEATES 180.5 pts | G.H.SLINN 156(187) |
| 1996 | G.H.KEATES | S.J.BUNN |
| 1997 | A.J.CARTER | A.J.CARTER |
| 1998 | A.J.CARTER | G.P.CONDON and A.P.WRAY |
| 1999 | A.J.LIMBERT | S.P.TOOTELL |
| 2000 | J.M.LLOYD | G.CONDON |
| 2001 | G.H.KEATES | A.J.CARTER |
| 2002 | | |
| 2003 | | |
| 2004 | | |
| 2005 | | |
| 2006 | | |
| 2007 | | |
| 2008 | | |
| 2009 | | |
| 2010 | | |
| 2011 | | |
| 2012 | | |

# CHAPTER 18

# The Golfer Trophy

"With the benefit of all the things I've learned now, I wish I was still in my prime"

Nick Faldo age forty three, prior to The Tiger Woods "Slam" at Augusta 2001 age twenty four.

**ONE of the surprises at trophies night is always who has won this trophy, since the winner is not actually announced until that evening. The trophy was presented in 1948 by an anonymous donor and is awarded to the winner returning the best three medal scores under handicap returned during the season. The three medals to count being nominated by the committee. Unlike the other trophy boards, the winning score is displayed.**

In 1969 Chris Westall upstaged his English International Junior mate Conrad Ceislewicz to win the trophy. In view of the format of the competition, it is not too surprising that no player has managed to win the trophy twice, possibly as a reduction in their handicaps. The fast running fairways during the year of the great drought suited Ray Moir's game when he became champion in 1976. At Kettering Road the lowest score was 186 by Richard Palmer, whereas at Harlestone, Derek Abel recorded 190 in a fine golf season. There was the first tie for the trophy in 1992 when Graham Castle and Adam Stevens could not be separated even after the use of the fourth card. The Peacock brothers Adrian & Martin became winners on the old and new courses in 1985 & 1991 respectively.

County players from the Club Jim Pettigrew, Alan Parker, Kevin Newman and Glenn Keates added this trophy to their own impressive lists of wins in 1973, 1977, 1980 and 2001 respectively.

You can imagine my fatherly pride, when at the Millennium trophies night my son Alex Izzard became the champion. As Bob Jones was delivering his description of the year's events, those assembled all expected Simon Freshwater to be the winner. There was a guarded level of confidence on his face, which changed rapidly. The surprised looks on Simon's and Alex's faces, the friendly glances exchanged will stay in my mind forever, during the few seconds after Bob had announced the result. This continued the recent trend of young and rapidly-improving golfers being successful in this competition, although some of the Club's old boys have managed to get their hands on the trophy in the past.

| Year | Name | Score | Year | Name | Score |
|------|------|-------|------|------|-------|
| 1948 | A.M.HARRISON | 212 | 1980 | K.NEWMAN | 199 |
| 1949 | J.H.BAXTER | 202 | 1981 | R.SWIFT | 193 |
| 1950 | R.L.CLARKE | 205 | 1982 | I.SMITH | 187 |
| 1951 | R.W.CLARKE | 199 | 1983 | R.PALMER | 186 |
| 1952 | M.R.CLARKE | 202 | 1984 | R.L.SLOAN | 193 |
| 1953 | R.G.HALLIDAY | 206 | 1985 | A.J.PEACOCK | 187 |
| 1954 | F.G.RIDDICK | 204 | 1986 | K.HEARD | 197 |
| 1955 | B.COOKSLEY | 206 | 1987 | C.MACKENZIE | 194 |
| 1956 | G.THOMSON | 206 | 1988 | T.R.ADDINGTON | 188 |
| 1957 | B.J.HALL | 201 | 1989 | R.G.BUSWELL | 187 |
| 1958 | R.L.CLARKE | 209 | 1990 | D.R.ABEL | 190 |
| 1959 | P.E.StQUINTON | 200 | 1991 | M.C.PEACOCK | 204 |
| 1960 | B.N.JONES | 195 | 1992 | G.D.CASTLE | |
| | | | | A.D.STEVENS | 204 |
| 1961 | P.E.StQUINTON | 205 | 1993 | C.HOPEWELL | 197 |
| 1962 | L.A.JOHNSON | 202 | 1994 | C.P.JOHNSON | 204 |
| 1963 | J.F.KNIGHT | 203 | 1995 | A.J.CARTER | |
| 1964 | M.J.CURWEN | 201 | 1996 | A.G.WEST | |
| 1965 | M.EVERITT | 206 | 1997 | G.CONDON | |
| 1966 | J.D.PRITCHARD | 202 | 1998 | A.P.WRAY | 197 |
| 1967 | C.CIESLEWICZ | 194 | 1999 | S.P.TOOTELL | |
| 1968 | A.B.HODDER | 199 | 2000 | A.J.IZZARD | |
| 1969 | C.S.WESTALL | 199 | 2001 | G.H.KEATES | 204 |
| 1970 | J.C.HUNTER | 201 | 2002 | | |
| 1971 | G.A.REDFERN | 200 | 2003 | | |
| 1972 | J.R.HURLEY | 202 | 2004 | | |
| 1973 | J.M.PETTIGREW | 197 | 2005 | | |
| 1974 | M.PARRY | 204 | 2006 | | |
| 1975 | P.BEEBY | | 2007 | | |
| 1976 | A.R.MOIR | | 2008 | | |
| 1977 | A.J.PARKER | | 2009 | | |
| 1978 | P.N.WHITE | 201 | 2010 | | |
| 1979 | P.BARRETT | 199 | 2011 | | |
| | | | 2012 | | |

# CHAPTER 19

# The Wellingborough Cup

"Golf tips are like asparin. One may do you some good, but if you swallow the whole bottle you will be lucky to survive"

Harvey Penick

THIS trophy came about in an unusual and special way. Subscribed by members of Wellingborough G.C. and presented to Northampton G.C. on the 16th September 1927. The presentation was in recognition of the generous gesture made by the committee of Northampton G.C. in 1926 when for some time their home course was closed owing to an outbreak of foot and mouth disease. Wellingborough members were invited to play at Kettering Road free of charge.

The cup was originally awarded to the player returning the best score over eighteen Holes bogey until 1989 when it changed to fourball betterball. The competition is played alternately on each course. In this foot and mouth year of 2001 the cup will be competed for appropriately at Wellingborough. Generous gestures of this nature strongly typify the spirit that exists within this wonderful game. This will be the first time that the competition will have been played on the Club's new greens, which have been completely rebuilt to provide a dryer surface. There have been two breaks in the competition in1988 and 1991 due to administrative issues. In 1998 the Cup was not played for because the Northampton members objected to the limited number of tee times available and withdrew.

The trophy was originally played for in singles bogey format but became a fourball Better ball event from 1989 onwards. This may explain why players with higher Handicaps have dominated the winner's enclosure recently, since scores of at least forty five stableford points have become the accepted norm. The low men do sometimes have their days, for example Northampton's Neil Frost and Gary Addington in 1993, Chris

Hopewell and Glenn Keates in 1994 and Wellingborough's Richard Brown and David Hunt in 1998. Since the format of the competition changed there has only been three Wellingborough winners, compared to nine winners from Northampton. A winning pair from Wellingborough was most appropriate, in the foot and mouth year of 2001.

| | | | |
|---|---|---|---|
| 1927 | R.S.JELLEYMAN +3 N | 1970 | W.L.BROWN +4 N |
| 1928 | G.N.SOMERS −2 N | 1971 | A.NORRIE +3 W |
| 1929 | F.ALIBONE -2 N* | 1972 | T.J.LUDLOW +3 N |
| 1930 | R.JUSTICE +2 N* | 1973 | J.C.HUNTER +3 N |
| 1931 | F.C.ROE -2 N | 1974 | D.MACDONALD N |
| 1932 | P.HUTTON all sqr N | 1975 | A.HARRISON +3 N |
| 1933 | H.J.D.ARKELL +1 N | 1976 | N.J.REDDEN W |
| 1934 | R.E.RUSHTON +1 N | 1977 | L.RUSSELL 39 pts N |
| 1935 | R.S.JELLEYMAN -3 N | 1978 | J.DILKES N |
| 1936 | P.HUTTON +2 N | 1979 | J.A.BROWN 40pts N |
| 1937 | J.H.MILLS all sqr N | 1980 | A.H.C.HART N |
| 1938 | C.S.CATLOW +3 N | 1981 | G.SMITH 42 pts N |
| 1939 | J.H.MILLS -1 N | 1982 | A.J.WALLBURTON N |
| 1940 | H.B.GRIFFIN -1 N | 1983 | M.J.RICHARDS 41 pts N |
| 1941 | A.J.FAULKNER -2 N | 1984 | L.EVERARD W |
| 1942 | C.S.CATLOW N | 1985 | D.A.DARE 39pts N |
| 1943 | C.S.CATLOW -2 N | 1986 | J.LOWRY 38pts W |
| 1944 | F.ALIBONE -1 N | 1987 | J.HALLWOOD N |
| 1945 | T.A.JEYES +3 N | 1988 | NO COMPETITION |
| 1946 | F.C.ROE N | 1989 | R.SOLOMAN |
| | | | R.W.GLASS 47pts N |
| 1947 | F.C.ROE -2 N* | 1990 | A.NORRIE |
| | | | K.TURNER W |
| 1948 | J.W.TAYLOR N | 1991 | NO COMPETITION |
| 1949 | J.E.GIFFIN N | 1992 | A.PANTER |
| | | | A.S.BOND 43pts N |
| 1950 | H.J.MERRY N | 1993 | N.J.FROST |
| | | | G.P.ADDINGTON N |
| 1951 | A.COKER N | 1994 | C.HOPEWELL |
| | | | G.H.KEATES 46 pts N |
| 1952 | A.GILDON N | 1995 | N.S.HANWELL |
| | | | R.E.CRADDOCK 46pts N |
| 1953 | R.J.PATTERSON N | 1996 | N.S.INWOOD |
| | | | D.LAIRD N |

| | | | |
|---|---|---|---|
| 1954 | R.S.MUMFORD -3 N | 1997 | C.NICHOLS C.COX N |
| 1955 | A.ANDERSON +1 N | 1998 | R.W.BROWN D.G.HUNT W |
| 1956 | N.JONES +3 N | 1999 | J.W.PETTS P.S.TAYLOR N |
| 1957 | F.G.RIDDICK -2 N | 2000 | I.P.ROBINS C.P.JOHNSON N |
| 1958 | B.J.HALL +4 N | 2001 | T.VEAL J.COWPER W |
| 1959 | R.H.EDWARDS +4 W | 2002 | |
| 1960 | H.OLLERTON +2 N | 2003 | |
| 1961 | J.H.EVANS +3 | 2004 | |
| 1962 | DR.P.BERMINGHAM +4 N | 2005 | |
| 1963 | L.A.JOHNSON +2 N | 2006 | |
| 1964 | L.P.CLARKE +3 N | 2007 | |
| 1965 | J.D.PRITCHARD all sqr N | 2008 | |
| 1966 | R.MATTHEWS +1 N | 2009 | |
| 1967 | F.C.COLES +1 W* | 2010 | |
| 1968 | C.R.CIESLEWICZ +3 N | 2011 | |
| 1969 | C.R.CIESLEWICZ +2 N* | 2012 | |

*Play Off
1929 A.J.Alibone Runner Up
1930 F.Garrard RU
1931 L.M.Allison RU
1947 W.H.Abbott & F.Garrard RUs
1967 E.C.Kottler RU
1969 C.J.Brydon RU

N Northampton    W Wellingborough

*Bob Glass and Dick Soloman dancing in the old clubhouse to celebrate winning the Hollingsworth Trophy and the Ryder Cup in 1987.*

# CHAPTER 20

# The Adams Hospital Cup

"Never bet with anyone you meet on the first tee, who has a deep suntan, a one iron in his bag and squinty eyes"

Dave Marr

**THIS trophy is competed for annually between Northampton and Kingsthorpe Golf Clubs since 1936 at both courses alternately. H.W.Adams presented the trophy originally, as the Hospital Cup. The choice of this name is unknown. The trophy is competed for as a singles competition played off handicap.**

Conrad Ceislewicz's fine form in 1969 continued as the youngster shot Nett 66 for victory. Richard Lovelady the Club Professional's son became the youngest ever winner with a fine score of Nett 65. The 1985 result involved a three-cornered play-off involving two Kingsthorpe players R.Adey, R.Cox and Northampton's Gavin Riddall. Gavin was initially forced to play off a handicap two lower than when he tied for the trophy and eventually lost by one shot. Following a letter to the Royal and Ancient, Gavin was declared the eventual winner by one shot. The trophy is not, however, engraved with his name on it!

Sadly the records for this trophy are incomplete, especially for those players who have actually won it.

| Year | Winner | Year | Winner |
|------|--------|------|--------|
| 1936 | E.GUILLAUME  KGC | 1969 | C.R.CEISLEWICZ 74-8=66 NGC |
| 1937 | A.L.WARD 74-6=68 NGC | 1971 | T.NEWMAN 81-20=61 NGC |
| 1938 | T.S.ROBINSON KGC | 1973 | R.LOVELADY 75-10=65 NGC |
| 1939 | W.SAVAGE NGC 90-22=68 | 1975 | R.WALKER 72-7=65 KGC |
| 1941 | W.H.CHAPMAN 93-20= 73 NGC | 1978 | R.WEBSTER 83-20=63 NGC |

| | |
|---|---|
| 1943 A.W.STEVENSON 85-15=70 KGC | 1980 R.D.JERVIS 81-13=63 KGC |
| 1944 R.WIGNALL KGC | 1982 R.BUSWELL 76-11=65 NGC |
| 1945 A.V.HEARN 87-20=67 | 1983 TIE* |
| 1953 R.C.ANDERSON NGC | 1984 S.L.McARTHUR 71-11=60 NGC |
| 1955 W.BAILEY 88-18=70 KGC | 1985 G.J.RIDDALL* NGC |
| 1957 G.BELL 93-27=66 | 1986 R.STANTON 73-10=73 KGC |
| 1959 J.GERARD 86-20=66* | 1988 B.J.OLLIVE 75-14=61 NGC |
| 1960 R.BOTWOOD NGC | 1991 L.BUTCHER 63 KGC |
| 1961 S.PANTHER 75-10=65 NGC | 1992 P.AMBIDGE 77-12=65 NGC |
| 1962 A.LYON NGC | 1994 G.TOOTELL 78-13=65 NGC |
| 1963 R.D.PURSER 85-17=68 NGC | 1998 G.G.THOMAS NGC |
| 1965 I.M.ASHBY 90-24=66 NGC | 1999 S.PERT KGC |
| 1966 S.S.ADAMS KGC | 2000 I.LOVELL 83-22=61 KGC |
| 1967 G.B.PYKE 80-12=68 NGC | 2001 D.J.SMITH KGC |

* Play Offs
1959 D.Savage Runner Up
1983 Tie W.Blundell, SMcDonald & J.Webster Nett 65 Winner Unknown
1985 R.Adey & R.Cox RUs

# CHAPTER 21

# Captain's Weekend

"Golf is like a love affair: If you don't take it seriously, it's not fun, if you do take it seriously, it breaks your heart"

Arnold Daly

THIS is always one of the highlights of the golfing year, which is often over-subscribed. In it's early days the venue was often at the seaside including such wonderful courses as Sheringham, Cromer, Royal West Norfolk and Skegness and top-drawer inland courses such as Ferndown, Woodhall Spa and St Pierre. More recently and possibly as a result of increased green fees, the attitude of the members at these top flight Club's and the popularity of the event, the venue has moved to nice courses which are able to accommodate at least fifty golfers from Thursday through to Sunday. I am certain that the choice of courses which is personally chosen by the Captain is only one element of what is always a great weekend. The new venues are in actual fact probably more suitable to the great diversity of handicaps which regularly attend this event. We have in the last few years witnessed handicaps from scratch to twenty six. Players tend to arrive at the venue on the Thursday and acclimatise themselves with the surroundings and course.

The betterball bogey competition is played on the Friday where several golfers have won the event on two occasions. These include Bill James, Sid Teckman, Ernie Potter, John Harwood, and Club Captains Ron Whittaker and Ron Halliwell et al. Ron Halliwell became the first ever winner of the Captain's Bogey and the betterball in 1984 at Skegness which was followed by Pete Huntley in 1996. Alf Lovelady, one of our loving professionals, lifted the trophy for the first Pro victory with Albert Hart in 1982 during Tony Stevens Captain's Weekend at Skegness. Paul Oakenfull is becoming the player one needs to play with for victory, since he became a three-

*Captain's Weekend 2001.*

times winner over a seventeen year period between 1984-2000. In 1999 brothers Martin and Adrian Peacock won father's and Captain Charles, Bogey tankard at the windy seaside course of North Shore Skegness.

The Saturday competition is usually a fourball betterball event, which is often coached for some golfers with a gentlemanly hangover from the previous evening's friendship and camaraderie following a lovely dinner. On such a weekend one could possibly feel that the golf is secondary to the other feelings which are generated at a venue where members relax in balmy surroundings with their friends. The pairings are determined on the Friday evening's post dinner draw, which always attracts much discussion later in the bar. I am sure the odd wager might be placed on which pair is likely to win. There have been some remarkable scores amassed in winning the competition. For example, Millenium winners John Pearson and Tom Heffernan recording a points tally of 47 Stableford points. Peter Beeby has become the partner to be with since he has been a winner four times. At Bramshaw in 1993 Derek Hoblin was so pleased to have won, he phoned his wife Cath to tell her. She listened to his very relaxed delivery and promptly put the phone down, assuming that "he was one over the eight and could not possibly have won". The 1996 weekend was notable, since one of our Senior members, Fred Perkins, won the long drive competition much to the embarrassment of the long and not so straight hitters. Last year at Forest Pines, during the presentation ceremony, Kevin Dickens entertained the members assembled with his marvellous rendition of Seve.

There have been a few holes in one on Captain's Weekend over the years; the latest one was achieved by Richard Craddock who aced the 6th hole at Forest Pines in 2001.

# BOGEY & FOURBALL BETTER BALL COMPETITION

## WINNERS 1951-2001

| YEAR | CAPTAIN | VENUE | BOGEY | BETTERBALL |
|------|---------|-------|-------|------------|
| 1951 | TED COKER | SHERINGHAM | W.TURNER B.A.MARBROOK | |
| 1952 | HORACE LACEY | SHERINGHAM | E.A.DIXON E.F.FULLER | |
| 1953 | BILL HUNTER | FERNDOWN | A.E.JONES & S.V.HEARN | |
| 1954 | D FISHER | BRANCASTER | E.F.FULLER & E.H.SMITH | |
| 1955 | BILL TURNER | WOODHALL SPA | M.D.ENGEL D.F.ROBINSON | |
| 1956 | JOHN EYTON-JONES | SKEGNESS | C.A.SPENCER D.R.THOM | |
| 1957 | RON LOWERY | SKEGNESS | D.R.THOM & L.FUCHS | |
| 1958 | HAROLD SHENFIELD | SKEGNESS | J.SHINE & A.COKER | |
| 1959 | FRANK SKETCHLEY | THORPNESS | S.J.MORTON J.SHINE | |
| 1960 | BOB CLARKE | WOODHALL SPA | R.S.MUMFORD D.W.BERRY | |
| 1961 | HOWARD GARDINER | SHERINGHAM | D.C.SOUTHEY& W.CHAPMAN | |
| 1962 | BILL CHAPMAN | CROMER | C.C.WESTON & R.PURSER | |

| YEAR | CAPTAIN | VENUE | BOGEY | BETTERBALL |
|------|---------|-------|-------|------------|
| 1963 | RAY BEIRNE | SHERINGHAM | P.BAMENT & R.PARTINGTON | |
| 1964 | DES SOUTHEY | CROMER | H.OLLERTON & J.NEEDHAM | |
| 1965 | CECIL WESTON | SKEGNESS | J.OATES & B.W.SCOTT | |
| 1966 | ERIC KOTTLER | SKEGNESS | F.SKETCHLEY & C.WRIGHT | |
| 1967 | ERIC DOUGLAS | SKEGNESS | R.MATTHEWS & J.HARRIS | |
| 1968 | JACK SHINE | SKEGNESS | N.A.HAVANT & J.W.JAMES | |
| 1969 | ALAN WESTLEY | SKEGNESS | G.B.PYKE & J.W.JAMES | |
| 1970 | JOE PYKE | WOODHALL SPA | H.BUCKENHAM & W.COWLEY | |
| 1971 | DON MONTGOMERY | CROMER | W.BOTWOOD D.GARLICK | |
| 1972 | CHARLES DURANT | SKEGNESS | S.TICKMAN & J.SHINE | |
| 1973 | FRANK MOSES | SKEGNESS | D.MONTGOMERY S.TECKMAN | |
| 1974 | JOHN GRIFFIN | SKEGNESS | R.E.BRACKLEY C.C.WESTON | |
| 1975 | HARRY OLLERTON | SKEGNESS | T.J.LUDLOW & C.J.TURNER | |
| 1976 | CHARLES BRYDEN | SKEGNESS | W.A.CLARKE & J.W.J.WOODS | |
| 1977 | JOHN HALLIWELL | ST PIERRE | R.NEWMAN & E.POTTER* | |
| 1978 | GLYNN COLES | ST PIERRE | D.TODD & P.WORTH | |
| 1979 | MAURICE JAFFA | ST PIERRE | A.F.STEVENS R.WHITTAKER | |
| 1980 | STAN COOK | ST PIERRE | T.K.JAMES & L.JARVIS | |
| 1981 | BRIAN PICKERELL | WOODHALL SPA | R.K.DICK & E.POTTER | |
| 1982 | TONY STEVENS | SKEGNESS | A.LOVELADY & A.H.HART | J.EYTON-JONES & ? |
| 1983 | KEN BILLINGHAM | SKEGNESS | J.HARWOOD & T.F.JONES | |

| YEAR | CAPTAIN | VENUE | BOGEY | BETTERBALL |
|------|---------|-------|-------|------------|
| 1984 | RON HALLIWELL | SKEGNESS | R.J.HALLIWELL P.OAKENFULL | |
| 1985 | BRIAN SMITH | TEWKSBURY | J.HARWOOD & M.SHELFORD | |
| 1986 | BRIAN MEADOWS | TELFORD | R.W.WHITTAKER & D.EVANS | |
| 1987 | ROGER STARMER | TEWKSBURY | P.BEEBY J.SINGLEHURST | P.BEEBY J.FELL 43 PTS |
| 1988 | BRIAN FROST | TEWKSBURY | R.J.HALLIWELL N.WHITE | R.NEWMAN T.JONES |
| 1989 | RON WHITTAKER | PATSHULL PARK | | B.SMITH P.HEATH |
| 1990 | DAVID PRIOR | PATSHULL PARK | G.GARBUTT A.D.YOUNGSON | |
| 1991 | BRIAN OLLIVE | MORETON HAMPSTEAD | G.KEATES B.J.OLLIVE | P.BEEBY M.CHAMBERLAIN 43 PTS |
| 1992 | KEITH PANTER | HARDELOT | R.J.STARMER R.WHITE | P.BEEBY C.PEACOCK 39 PTS |
| 1993 | GEOFF GARBUTT | BRAMSHAW | | P.BEEBY D.HOBLIN 41 PTS |
| 1994 | TREVOR LLOYD | SKEGNESS | J.MALIN R.WHITE | |
| 1995 | BOB FROST | BRAMSHAW | S.EBORALL K.HEARD | S.EBORALL P. HUNTLEY 41 PTS |
| 1996 | PETER HUNTLEY | PATSHALL PARK | P.R.HUNTLEY P.OAKENFULL | |
| 1997 | BEN MIDDLETON | HAWKSTONE PARK | M.S.SMITH T.J.PANTHER | K.DICKENS N.INWOOD |
| 1998 | MARTIN SMITH | MEON VALLEY | D.C.PRIOR C.S.NICKELS | |
| 1999 | CHARLES PEACOCK | SKEGNESS | A.J.PEACOCK M.C.PEACOCK | T.LLOYD P.G.HIAMS 44 pts |
| 2000 | TONY HARRISON | BREADSALL PRIORY | D.DARE P.OAKENFULL | J.PEARSON 47 pts T.HEFFERNAN |
| 2001 | GEOFF KEATES | FOREST PINES | M.J.IZZARD R.L.JONES 41 pts | R.L.JONES J.PETTS |

* Derek Holland & Ken Billingham claim to have won it!

*"Hey Kevin, let me tell you about my round."*
*"Oh go on then Pete, I'm all ears."*

# CHAPTER 22

# County Connections
# and Winners

"I've always made a total effort, even when the odds seemed entirely against me. I never quit trying; I never felt that I didn't have a chance to win"

Arnold Palmer

The Club has throughout its entire history had a long and close association with the Northamptonshire Golf Union. In fact the Club has provided officials, players and County champions since the formation of the N.G.U. in 1921. The Club has the unique distinction of providing Secretaries to the Union for a period of seventy-two years, where great stalwarts such as G.A.T. "Tubby" Vials, Frank Wild, Charles Catlow, amongst others have administered the Union's affairs. During the last thirty years we have seen our now Club President Tom (T.C.A.) Knight and Tony Stevens as joint Secretaries between the years of 1979–1989. What a dynamic duo they became where most requests where met with the customary response of a throaty "HUMM" or "another waste of time". It was not always easy for young players to appreciate the "knife-like wit" expounding from the dynamic duo's tongues. Such lengthy and valued service resulted in Tony Stevens being elected as County President in 1990.

The County A and B teams compete for the Anglian League shields against Cambridgeshire, Leicestershire, Lincolnshire, Norfolk and Suffolk, where Club members have made a valuable contribution especially in the winning years of 1972, 1980 and 1990. The matches are played on Sundays when the eight-man teams play four foursomes in the morning and eight singles in the afternoon following a practice round the previous day. The Anglian League was formed in 1968 and the first blow was struck by Northamptonshire's player Richard Catlow who was playing with former Club member and brother-in-law Richard Aitken at Thorpness G.C. on Sunday the 13th April 1969. The ball apparently finished in a bush! The league has been largely dominated by Leicestershire and Lincolnshire. Cambridgeshire became the last County to feature as winners when they finally won the A Shield in 2001 .

*The winning Anglian League B Team 1980. Left to Right: A. M. S. Lord, J. M. Payne, R. Haig, N. B. Highfield (Capt.), M. J. Izzard, P. Scott, K. V. Newman, D. Evans.*

Northamptonshire won the A trophy in 1972, where club member Jim Pettigrew was Northampton's lone representative, together with former members Richard Aitken and Conrad Ceislewicz.

My early experiences with the B Team included the famous Felixstowe weekend of 1978, which featured three players from the Club. The team had travelled down to Felixstowe Ferry G.C. on the Saturday for a practice round on a golf course, which has a road running through it. The opening shot was played by Chris Westall, which flew like a duck straight through the windscreen of a Mini! The heavily-tattooed driver was soon striding up the fairway and offered to put the ball where the sun does not shine. Fortunately for Chris, the Club and County officers present rapidly resolved this charged situation. Walter Clarke played superbly in the afternoon, going round in level par for a halved match. My own

*President Tom Knight, Captain Brian Frost, Sue Minton (Carlsberg), Stuart Brown and Past President Harold Shenfield with the Mermaid Trophy at the N.G.U. Open 1988.*

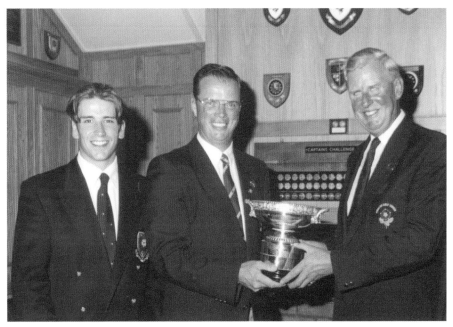

*Glenn Keates and Gary Wolstenholme with E.G.U. President John Scrivener at Woodhall Spa 1998.*

91

*County Champion 1998 Glen Keates with proud parents Geoff and Judy.*

contribution included a chip in for an eagle and putting Chris Westall's fiancée in hospital! Even though I was second to tee-off on the long par five sixth hole my 300-yard drive hit the unfortunate caddie straight between the shoulder blades on the fly. She went down like a stone, I thought I had killed her! She was in fact quite all right, though badly bruised and shaken after a trip to the Casualty Department. I have never felt so guilty and eventually lost three and two on that memorable July weekend. I can empathise with Jon Lloyd some thirteen years later (see Chapter 1)!

The B team shield was won for the first and only time in 1980 when the team won the first four matches to seal victory. The team was captained by the Daventry schoolteacher and character Barry Highfield who kept us all in line! The author, Bob Killip and Kevin Newman were members of the sixteen-man squad, which recorded the following results.

| | |
|---|---|
| Leicestershire at Scraptoft G.C. | Won 7.5/4.5 |
| Cambridgeshire at Kettering G.C. | Won 9/3 |
| Suffolk at Aldeburgh G.C. | Won 6.5/5.5 |
| Norfolk at Barnham Broom G.C. | Won 7/5 |
| Lincolnshire at Staverton Park G.C. | Lost 9/3 |

| Player | Matches | Foursome Wins | Singles Wins | % Victories |
|---|---|---|---|---|
| B.HIGHFIELD *D* | 5 | 3 | 3 | 60 |
| R.HAIG *NC* | 5 | 4 | 3 | 67 |
| M.J.IZZARD *N* | 5 | 3.5 | 4 | 77 |
| P.SCOTT *KI* | 4 | 1.5 | 2.5 | 54 |
| S.MCDONALD *KI* | 4 | 2.5 | 1 | 38 |
| K.NEWMAN *N* | 3 | 2.5 | 0 | 28 |
| D.EVANS *NC* | 3 | 1 | 2 | 56 |
| I.MARSHALL *W* | 2 | 1 | 1 | 50 |
| M.HADDON *KI* | 2 | 2 | 2 | 100 |
| R.KILLIP *N* | 1 | 1 | 0 | 33 |
| M.SCOTT *PH* | 1 | 0 | 0 | 0 |
| R.HALL *KE* | 1 | 1 | 1 | 100 |
| N.GRIMMITT *W* | 1 | 1 | 0 | 33 |
| J.ELLIS *PM* | 1 | 0 | 1 | 67 |
| J.PAYNE *KE* | 1 | 0 | 0.5 | 33 |
| A.LORD *NC* | 1 | 0 | 0 | 0 |

*D* Daventry, *KE* Kettering, *KI* Kingsthorpe, *N* Northampton, *NC* Northants County, *PH* Priors Hall, *PM* Peterborough Milton, *W* Wellingborough.

County Champion 1999 and
2001, Nick Soto, our 'adopted'
Champion.

Alex Izzard, County Boys
Champion 2000

*N.G.U. County Dinner 1990 at Harlestone. Local, Regional and English Dignitaries. Left to Right: Gordon Upwood, Mike McMahon, Jack Humphries, Austin Harrup, Tony Stevens N.G.U. President, A. Bradford E.G.U., Mike Cooksey M.G.U., John Flanders M.G.U.*

*Anglian League Champions 1990. Left to Right: John Evans, Ian Marshall, Ian Achurch, Peter Flude, Darren Jones, Tony Stevens, Michael Pask, Dick Biggin, Martin Izzard and John Wilson.*

*Northampton's County Union Trophy winners 1998. Left to Right: G. H. Keates, County Champion, A. Field, Seniors Nett, J. C. Jones and A. J. Limbert Stableford Cup, D. J. Jessup + G.H.K. & A.J.L. Champion Club, A. J. & M. J. Izzard Family Foursomes.*

During the season there were numerous incidents which caused hilarity. At Aldeburgh, despite retiring early, the author was dragged out of bed at 1 a.m. since, those assembled in the bar decided it was his round! At Barnham Broom, Kevin Newman and David (The Boil) Evans threw one of the waitresses into the swimming pool fully-clothed because she was hot! Captain Barry had a certain and unique way of motivating us, we all found out quickly if boys being boys went too far. I shall always remember him getting up from his single room at Aldeburgh to give David Evans a short sharp, "Get to bed boyo", as he had overstepped the line. Barry was one of life's genuine characters who captained the side for a record eight years between 1976 and 1983 and became President of the Union in 1985. He became part of the fabric of Daventry Golf Club, where everyone knew him and could probably tell you a story with him in it! He was that sort and is sadly missed.

It was another ten years before Northamptonshire captured its next Anglian title the A team shield in 1990 after an eighteen-year wait. The details of this have been well documented in the NGU 2000 yearbook[2]. The annual County dinner was held at the Club that year, where the trophy was displayed, much to the pleasure of all concerned.

The dinner flowed beautifully along with the wine, port and brandy and also produced the famous, "No Petrol", story. The author had arranged to stay in Northampton and managed to obtain a lift with Peter Flude. Those who knew Peter would understand that he was a quiet character who had a wicked sense of humour if one got to know him. As we were both slightly inebriated (I think) he decided to drive around the town in his magnificent white Ford XR2i to avoid any complications. As we were heading past Delapre Golf Complex at fine speed and chatting about what a fine season it had become, Peter turned to me with horror in his eyes and said simply," No Petrol". The car very soon ground to a halt on the A45 dual carriageway somewhere close to the Barnes Meadow flyover. There was nothing for it; the dinner-jacketed author had to push the car! As we slowly made our way towards Bells Garage I was filled with relief and worry when the "jam sandwich" turned up to assist us. The officer was most obliging and took Peter off to obtain a can of petrol, what conversation occurred during the journey to and from the petrol station is now lost in the history of time since Peter is sadly no longer with us.

On the playing side Northampton have in the last thirty years produced many trophy winners, most notably the two County Champions, Richard Aitken and Glenn Keates, in 1968 and 1998 respectively. Richard moved to Northants County in 1969 and succeeded in retaining the Championship. He is a familiar figure on the County scene and continues to win trophies to this day. As County Champion Glenn played in the English Champion of Champions tournament at Woodhall Spa, where he finished a very creditable third behind winner, English International Gary

Wolstenholme, from neighbouring Leicestershire Club, Kilworth Springs. Woodhall Spa is an extremely demanding course, especially off the back tees at 7047 yards. Wolstenhome's first round of 67 was a course record, which stunned the players present, since he is not noted as a long hitter. Forty one year old Gary, became the English Champion of Champions for the fourth time in 2001 again at Woodhall Spa, where his two round total of 139 (68,71), reduced his handicap to a magnificent plus five, no amateur in Great Britain can match that. Can you imagine standing on the first tee, knowing that you have to add five to the number of strokes taken to obtain your nett score! I bet he does not play in the monthly medal!

As a result of Glenn Keates's, Dominic Jessup's and Andy Limbert's performance in the 1998 County Championship they went on to represent Northamptonshire at Northumberland Golf Club in the English Champion Club Tournament. The players were ably supported by Club Captain Martin Smith and finished with a total medal score of 309. This put them in 27th out of 33 playing Counties, above last team Caldy, from Cheshire on 316 and below winners Moor Park, Hertfordshire on 287. Andy Limbert's final seventeenth and eighteenth holes included an "illegal" drop from the six foot horse railings, according to E.G.U officials, and a five-putt on a very sloping final green, both of which did not in fact alter the final total, despite Andy's short lived personal embarrassment.

Northampton Golf Club effectively "retained" the County Championship when our adopted "scratch bar-man" Nick Soto won the title at Cold Ashby G.C. with scores of 69,71 two under par in 1999. Junior member and "talisman" Simon Freshwater was once again on the bag to complete a trio of caddying victories. I know that Northants County has a completely different point of view since he is a member there. Nick also became Champion in 2001 with a fine score of 71,70 one under par at Peterborough Milton narrowly beating the holder Adam Print by one shot to complete a hat-trick of victories for Northants County. Glenn Keates became County Match-play Champion in 2000 when he defeated Matt Peacock of Peterborough Milton Golf Club by a single hole in the 36 hole final at Staverton Park in a closely-fought contest. I am certain that the caddying skills of Messrs Lloyd and Izzard senior must have helped on this cold, wet and windy day.

Club members have featured well in the Stableford Cup with singles champions Harry Redman in 1970, Brian Ollive in 1988 and Jeff Moorcroft in 1989. The format of the competition changed in 1995 and produced pairs winners of Adrian Peacock and myself in 1997 at Kettering golf club. Club members Jim Campbell-Jones and Andy Limbert were watching from the veranda as Adrian stroked in a thirty-foot birdie putt for victory. Two chip-ins in the morning and afternoon rounds also helped to ensure a one-point victory. Adrian's birdie must have inspired Jim and Andy since they went on to win the trophy the following year at Wellingborough.

The Seniors Championship has seen Club members Harvey Richards, John Haddon (78 gross play-off against Jim Dalton) and John Harwood lift the gross trophy in 1982,1987 and 1989 respectively. In this memorable year of 1989 John Harwood also featured strongly in the Inaugural Great Britain and Ireland Clerical and Medical Golf Tournament at St Mellion, finishing in ninth place. This was in fact the first competition to be played on this demanding though beautiful course. The Senior's Nett trophy has been won recently by Neville Kny in 1997 and Austin Field in 1998.

The Club has featured fairly well recently in the Family Foursomes trophy with brothers Gary and Tony Addington in 1990, Charles and Joan Peacock in 1995 on a damp day at Kettering and myself and Alex Izzard also on a damp day at Kingsthorpe in 1998. There were many Northampton players taking part at Oundle G.C. in 1996 where the donor of the trophies H.W.Colton President (1957-8) of the Northamptonshire Golf Union kindly turned up to present his donated trophies on it's fortieth outing. Northampton G.C. only managing a third place that year.

Alex Izzard became the County Boys Champion in 2000 following a lengthy gap of thirty years behind club members and great players Conrad Ceislewicz in 1971&2 and Tim Giles in 1973 to ensure at last, a long overdue victory for the Junior section. Perhaps we shall not have to wait so long next time if new Junior Organiser and past Club Champion Jon Lloyd can rally the Juniors to greater heights.

*County Trophies won in the Millennium Year. Left to Right: A. J. Izzard, Boys Champion, Scratch League Division 2 G. P. Addington, Team Captain, G. H. Keates Match Play Champion.*

# CHAPTER 23

# The Hollingsworth Trophy

"Few moments can match this, I hope you young people realise that. It is a special moment that may never come again". Hale Irwin, Ryder Cup Kiawah Island 1991.

We were fortunate to hear Hale Irwin's guiding words as a true gentlemen at Kiawah Island, some players listened and some ignored those wise words, as normal!

*Jon Lloyd in action during the 1996 Hollingsworth Final.*

THE Club has always wanted to win this magnificent trophy which past Club President Bill Hollingsworth donated in 1955, the year I was born and when he was County Golf Union President. Bill Hollingsworth made a very significant contribution to the local golf scene and was twice County President in 1955 and 1967 and Club President between 1964-1982. The format of five foursomes played to a result is very conducive to generating team spirit and a true test of nerves. Bill Hollingsworth had a great passion for the game and was even playing golf in his nineties. Since his death in 1981 at the age of ninety four the trophy has been presented at the post-match meal by his daughter Mary Bird. A feeling for Bill's passion for the game can be felt from the letters he typed concerning the arrangements for the finals and the warmth in the letters of the scores returned to the Union by Club administrators (page 102 & 103).

The details of the competition were defined for our time of focus as: -

# HOLLINGSWORTH TROPHY 1969

The two sections shall comprise the following clubs: -

| A | B |
|---|---|
| Northants County | Kingsthorpe |
| Kettering | Peterborough |
| Northampton | Corby |
| Daventry | Wellingborough |
| Oundle | Rushden |

The individual matches shall be played as follows, the first named club in each instance will be the home Club: -

| A | B |
|---|---|
| Northants County v Oundle | Kingsthorpe v Peterborough |
| Kettering v Northants County | Peterborough v Corby |
| Daventry v Northants County | Corby v Kingsthorpe |
| Northants County v Northampton | Kingsthorpe v Wellingborough |
| Northampton v Daventry | Rushden v Kingsthorpe |
| Oundle v Northampton | Peterborough v Wellingborough |
| Northampton v Kettering | Rushden v Peterborough |
| Daventry v Kettering | Corby v Rushden |
| Kettering v Oundle | Wellingborough v Corby |
| Oundle v Daventry | Wellingborough v Rushden |

The rules governing the competition are: -

1. If more than five Clubs enter the President of the County Union shall divide them into two groups.
2. Clubs shall meet each other in the same group each year, the home team in each instance being drawn by the President (and shown first above).
3. If groups are formed, the leading Club in each group shall play off the final on a neutral course to be fixed by the President of the County Union.
4. The matches shall be foursomes, played off handicap (3/8 of difference of combined handicaps). Each game shall be played to a result. If necessary a game shall continue after the 18th hole until a decisive result is obtained, strokes being taken as in the first round.

Each side shall consist of five couples, and each match shall consist of five matches.

5. One point shall be scored for a win in each individual game. Any team not playing a full side will grant a win to the opposing team for each individual game so scratched. Should two or more clubs win the same number of matches , the tie shall be settled by the individual games won.

6. Matches shall be played between 1st April and 6th August, in evenings or on Saturday or Sunday afternoons, on dates to be mutually agreed by the Clubs involved (It is hoped that matches will be completed by mid-July).

7. Sheltering is permitted. Matches postponed due to inclement weather to be played in full within 21 days of the original date.

8. Clubs to be represented by full playing members only, playing off their handicap at that Club. No player may play for more than one Club in one season.

9. Any differences of opinion or dispute shall be settled by the President of the County Union or his nominee.

10. Each competing Club shall pay an entrance fee for the year of one pound five shillings.

11. The result of each match shall be notified in detail by letter to the Secretary of the County Union within seven days.

W.H.Abbott. Hon. Secretary 1st November 1968

*Hollingsworth Trophy winners 1978. Left to Right (back): R. Newman, H. R. Bierne, A. J. Parker, C. S. Westall, R. Swann, T . J. Ludlow, K.V. Newman. (Front): R. Mathews, Bill Hollingsworth, Glynn Coles (Club Captain), R.J.C. Killip, J.W. Halliwell*

# NORTHAMPTON GOLF CLUB

W. HOLLINGSWORTH,
"Sans Souci,"
10 Watersmeet,
Northampton. *Nov 2 56*
Phone 34207 or 34579

Dear Richard,

Thankyou for your letter.        Please do not worry about the fact that I did not know the result of the Handicap Foursomes.

My main concern is, of course, to have the Final where we can be assured of a suitable meal, and I feel you could not located us better than with Mrs Fogg's cuisine, which we have many times enjoyed.        Kettering, too must be the ideal venue for this year's Finalists.

Here I should mention that my hearing (forgive the pun) is so bad that I cannot use the telephone - hence my writing to you now !  -  and, by the way , I have to type, because my hands will not operate more than a word or two with the pen.

If you agree, Mary will take up the arrangements with Mrs Fogg, after I have invited the Captains with their Teams.        Can you please give me the name of the Captain of Peterborough Milton.

So, I would like to have a word with you when we get something to work on.

Please understand that I do not encroach on the arrangements other than the Meal, and, once we know the acceptors, I would appreciate your help on who else we can find room for.        Meantime, will you, if necessary, ring my Private Secretary - Mary ?

Cheerio,

*Letter from Bill Hollingsworth concerning the Final arrangements, typed at the age of 90. A great man.*

102

**DAVENTRY SCHOOL**
Headmaster : **D. J. P. WEAVER**, M.A.
**ASHBY ROAD, DAVENTRY**
Telephone Daventry 2387

**SAWBRIDGE
HOUSE**

Housemaster : **N. B. HIGHFIELD**, A.T.D.
Housemistress : **Mrs. W. SMITH**, B.Sc.

3ᵗʰ June 1976

Dear Richard

Here is the Hollingsworth Trophy record for Daventry Golf Club.

Thurs 20ᵗʰ May — Daventry beat Northants County    4 . 1

Thurs 27 May — Daventry beat Kingsthorpe    4 1

Thurs 3ʳᵈ June — Daventry lost to Rushden    1 . 4

Thurs 17ᵗʰ June — Daventry lost to Priors Hall    2 . 3 .

Hope you had an enjoyable holiday.

Yours.

Barry.

*Letter from Barry Highfield to County Secretary Richard Catlow on Daventry's performance in the Trophy.*

As the number of Clubs in the Union has grown over the years, so has the number of teams competing for this wonderful trophy. From the original ten teams in 1969 we now have twenty-four teams competing in 2001. Bill would have been proud.

The Club has been fortunate to win this trophy in 1978, 1983, 1987, 1988 and 1996. The details of all these victories apart from 1996 are documented in Gil Sibley's superb book, "A Centenary History 1893-1993". The 1978 final was played for the first and only time as a three-way contest where we successfully defeated Kettering and Daventry on October 1st. The post match celebrations were punctuated by a race to the fifth green from the clubhouse at half past twelve dressed in suits. Team captain Tony Stevens positioned his car near the first tee and then drove his car up and down the hills and hollows with headlights full on to help former professional footballer Ron Newman and Nick Durant with their vision. The race was won easily by Ron since Nick fell over several times and discharged the contents of the match meal and wine. The real winner of the race was in fact a long distance runner who had joined the post match celebrations. Both Ron and Nick fancied their chances of beating him. Speaking to Nick recently he believes that he would now win if it were restaged, since Ron is now in his senior years and not quite the fit footballer from 1978! Tony Stevens gave them a lift back to the clubhouse after their exertions to rejoin the celebrations and collect their winnings from the various bets, which had been placed!

The trophy returned to its traditional format the following year since it was felt that playing foursomes in sixes did not really work for those clubs in Northamptonshire. We lost the 1982 final at Church Brampton G.C. and unbeknown to many Tony Stevens actually provided the Champagne for the winning team. At this time the club did not serve champagne, forward thinking Tony Stevens had taken a case with him to the final for Northampton's hopeful celebration. Since the result went the "other way" the case was generously donated to Kettering G.C. by a man with a great love of the game. The nineteen eighties proved to be a vintage period for the club where we played in five finals and won the trophy in 1983,1987 and 1988. Alex Izzard was present at the 1983 final at the tender age of two months, being carried around the course by his mother. If we qualify for the 2001 final he could argue that he has been a serving member for eighteen years! Sadley the final was to see the last view for Northampton players of the promising player Robbie Cantwell son of the famous local footballer Noel Cantwell, who tragically died at a tender age. There is a plaque on the shelter by the end of the par three ninth hole at Peterborough Milton G.C. in memory of a fine young man. Every time I pass this plaque, I warmly look back and remember seeing his dashing locks and flamboyant mannerisms from the 1983 final.

The Northampton team has always experienced great support, from the members and player's families, where the large crowds have often inspired us to victory often as the underdogs. The 1987 final at Peterborough Milton were memorable since Europe won the Ryder Cup for the first time on American soil as we were enjoying the presentation meal. In fact the meal was temporarily suspended until Seve Ballesteros sunk the winning putt on the seventeenth green against Curtis Strange. Captain Tony Jacklin's words, "This is the best day of my life", were being echoed across the Atlantic in a little wooden clubhouse on Kettering Road, Northampton.

We retained the trophy the following year in style against favourites Peterborough Milton at Church Brampton, where David Dare holed out from a bunker on the fifteenth hole for victory. In 1992 it looked as though we might progress to the final, however Nigel Harris's snapped putter on the thirteenth hole at Collingtree in the semi final probably decided our fate. In 1995 we were narrowly defeated by old rivals Kingsthorpe 3/2 at Kettering prior to them winning the trophy. Whilst we held a dominant position in the 1980's, Kingsthorpe and to a lesser extent Kettering have dominated the finals in the 1990's.

The Peterborough thread continued as we found that we were due to play them in 1996 on the 6th October and surprisingly overwhelmed them 5-0. Club Captain Peter Huntley had supported us all year; this must have made his year complete. This was long awaited pay back from the 1981 final where we were similarly dispatched 5-0. Northampton's passage to the final was achieved by the following results as described by long serving and committed Captain, Gary Addington: -

*Hollingsworth Trophy winners 1987. Left to Right: J.T. Haddon, G. P. Addington, M. J. Izzard, M. Britten, J.J. Hallwood, K. Billingham (Selector), A. J. Linney, P. M. H. Rees, A. J. Parker, R.J. Starmer (Club Captain), D.A. Dare.*

| | | |
|---|---|---|
| Cherwell Edge | Away | Won 5-0 |
| Staverton Park | Home | Won 5-0 |
| Kettering | Away | Lost 5-0 |
| Delapre Park | Home | Won 4-1 |

**Semi-Final**

Collingtree Park at Staverton Park　　　　　Won 4.5 to 0.5

**Final**

Peterborough Milton at Church Brampton　　Won 5-0


NORTHAMPTON　PETERBOROUGH MILTON

M.J.Izzard　　　　　J.Dyson　　　　　Won 6&4
G.H.Keates　　　　　I.Kerr

Once again a strong performance from the premier pair who were two over par when they completed a five out of five season.

A.J.Carter　　　　　M.Herson　　　　　Won 2&1
A.J.Peacock　　　　　M.Peacock

A poor start from Andy and Adrian as a result of Adrian's jetlag was forgotten when they found their best form on the back nine to complete a clean sweep in four matches.

S.P.Tootell　　　　　J.Ellis
J.M.Lloyd　　　　　G.MacDonald　　Won @ 20th

Although three down with five to play the young guns fought back to win. Jon's three wood on to the seventeenth green from a short drive, together with his tee shot on eighteen were possibly the shots of the final considering the pressure and anticipation of the day.

G.P.Addington (Capt)　　R.Cole　　　　　Won 2 Up
N.J.Frost　　　　　M.Humphries

A very up and down game eventually saw Gary and Neil win on the eighteenth as a result of Neil's straight driving and Gary's putting. The only pair to play six matches. Gary broke a club in the trees on the seventeenth after Neil's only wayward drive.

D.J.Jessup　　　　　I.Symonds　　　　Won 3&2
A.J.Limbert　　　　　N.Presto

Dominic and Andy were four up after five and never looked back where they were unbeaten that season together in three matches.

*A worried team, David Dare, captain Gary Addington and Neil Frost, discuss the current state of the match during the 1996 Hollingsworth Final.*

As the players, supporters and officials retired to the clubhouse at Harlestone it was music to the ear when after the ringing of the Club bell, Vice Captain Ben Middleton announced, "Gentlemen the free bar is now open". Most players did not arrive at work until Monday lunchtime following the friendly and lengthy celebrations.

*107*

We have a great relationship with the Peterborough team and have enjoyed their company on many occasions where we often have played after-match-meal golf with them. Incidents such as a throwing competition from the ladies sixteenth tee at Harlestone (won by Andy Carter), long driving competitions and a five iron challenge have taken place. Who can forget Peterborough player Jimmy Ellis chipping in with a five iron from the eighteenth tee at Milton on to the first green. Just visualise it the next time you are there and consider the degree of difficulty, the shot appears impossible but did actually happen on a sunny evening at PMGC!

In that memorable season of 1996 the players performances were: -

| Player | Played | Won | Halved | Lost | Percentage | Points |
|--------|--------|-----|--------|------|------------|--------|
| G.H.Keates | 5 | 5 | 0 | 0 | 100 | 5 |
| A.J.Carter | 4 | 4 | 0 | 0 | 100 | 4 |
| D.J.Jessup | 3 | 3 | 0 | 0 | 100 | 3 |
| J.M.Lloyd | 3 | 3 | 0 | 0 | 100 | 3 |
| S.J.Bailey | 1 | 1 | 0 | 0 | 100 | 1 |
| M.J.Izzard | 6 | 5 | 0 | 1 | 83.3 | 5 |
| A.J.Limbert | 5 | 4 | 0 | 1 | 80 | 4 |
| G.Addington | 6 | 4 | 1 | 1 | 75 | 4.5 |
| N.J.Frost | 6 | 4 | 1 | 0 | 75 | 4.5 |
| S.P.Tootell | 4 | 3 | 0 | 0 | 75 | 3 |
| D.A.Dare | 4 | 3 | 0 | 0 | 75 | 3 |
| A.J.Peacock | 6 | 4 | 0 | 0 | 67 | 4 |
| K.Heard | 3 | 2 | 0 | 0 | 67 | 2 |
| C.I.Mackenzie | 2 | 1 | 0 | 0 | 50 | 1 |
| G.J.Riddall | 1 | 0 | 0 | 0 | 0 | 0 |
| J.J.Varco | 1 | 0 | 0 | 1 | 0 | 0 |

For the record, the following semi and final performances were recorded by the club's team between 1969 and 2001:-

| Year | Semi-Final | Team | Final | Team |
|------|-----------|------|-------|------|
| 1978 | Not Contested | NA | Won 3/2 | Daventry |
| | | | Won 4/1 | Kettering |
| 1981 | Won 3/2 | Kingsthorpe | Lost 5/0 | Peterborough Milton |
| 1982 | Won 3/2 | Peterborough Milton | Lost 3/2 | Kettering |
| 1983 | Won 3/2 | Church Brampton | Won 4/1 | Peterborough Milton |

| 1987 | Won 3/2 | Kingsthorpe | Won 4/1 | Priors Hall |
|------|---------|-------------|---------|-------------|
| 1988 | Won 3/2 | Daventry | Won 3.5/1.5 | Peterborough Milton |
| 1992 | Lost 3/2 | Kettering | - | - |
| 1995 | Lost 3/2 | Kingsthorpe | - | - |
| 1996 | Won 4.5/0.5 | Collingtree Park | Won 5/0 | Peterborough Milton |
| 1999 | Lost 4.5/0.5 | Collingtree Park | - | - |
| 2001 | Lost 3/2 | Priors Hall | - | - |

The 2001 Hollingsworth campaign saw the Club make it in to the semi final from the County Union's Group B qualifier, where the team won all five of the qualifying matches. The final qualifying game was played away at Cherwell Edge G.C. where we had to win the match or Staverton Park G.C. would have progressed to the semi-final on "goal difference". The team won three matches to two when "THE BEST EVER PAR IN THE HISTORY OF THE CLUB" was recorded, which included a fresh air shot and a shank.

Standing on the 260 yard par four seventh tee, ten handicapper Paul.M.F.Tee had a complete fresh air shot where the ball simply fell off the tee. Having consulted the rules book, the opposition declared that the ball must be played as it lies. Having removed the tee peg from the ground, playing partner Alex Izzard bashed a three wood down close to the green. Paul was obviously in a slight state of shock and consequently shanked the ball which somehow managed to finish on the green. "One Jab" Alex Izzard then proceeded to hole the thirty foot putt across a sloping green for an extremely unlikely half in four. The pair going on from this unbelievable happening to record a victory by 4/2 and to collect one of the three points the team won to ensure victory. Their opponents made many friendly though frustrated references to this fluke during the post match meal.

This was not to be the end for PMFT's day as he decided to have a lift back to the Club in one of the Club's flying machines as part of a race back to Harlestone to celebrate. Sitting in the front of a car, which was reputedly travelling at 150 mph which was being pursued by two members cars travelling at the paltry speed of 148 mph the driver stated don't worry Paul it's limited at 155 mph.

Paul simply said, "Good", in a frightened tone.

I had personally taken the country route back to the Club with Alex since the sun was setting from the west. The beautiful golden ochre and sandstone colours on the shapely and spacious houses in Northamptonshire villages such as Moreton Pinkney, Canons Ashby and Litchborough made me realise how good life can be where simple things like team spirit, camaraderie and friendship are what golf and life is all about. We saw on the journey home a Northamptonshire Owl, strictly known in birding circles as the Little Owl, which was introduced to England by the famous Northamptonshire Naturalist from Oundle Lord Lillford in 1889. The Little Owl is the symbol of the ornithological publication "The Birds of Northamptonshire" which has been published annually since 1969 the very year that I joined our great golf club and submitted my first ever bird record. As a Naturalist & Golfer this is a publication I still contribute records to especially from Harlestone with such species as Whimbrel, Red Kite, Mandarin Duck and Nuthatch. We arrived at the Club ten minutes after the boy racers, that's why I drive a slower car which allows me to see more!

For the record the other qualifiers were from Group A Daventry who also won five matches out of five. Interestingly though strange, Northants County from group A lost all five matches! On paper they have the strongest squad of low handicap players anywhere in the County. Perhaps they are building a team for the future challenge of Northamptonshire's premier team trophy? Peterborough Milton G.C. from Group C also won five matches out of five, together with Priors Hall who won four matches out of four in Group D. In fact all of the teams in the semi-final were unbeaten. Looking back now on how we made it through to the semi final, Glenn Keates's and Alex Izzard's sudden death victory, at our par three twenty-third hole was probably the key point. This ensured victory by 3/2 against Staverton Park, our closest challengers.

The semi-finals were played at Kettering and Oundle G.C's on a very warm June Sunday where temperatures reached twenty-nine degrees Centigrade, with no breeze. Sadly we were to exit the competition at this vital stage losing by three matches to two against Priors Hall at Kettering Golf Club.

It was a very emotional semi-final. We were always likely to lose the first and fifth matches where both pairs of Glenn Keates and Alex Izzard, Dominic Jessup and Andy Limbert rapidly became three down and never looked like coming back. The golfers in the middle three matches staged a great revival from a poor start and after twelve holes stood at one down, two up and four up. If we could turn the second game around we might just win. When Jon Lloyd, in game two, holed from the back on the sixteenth hole for a classic birdie three on the stroke one 455 yard sixteenth hole, for a fighting victory by three and two, those assembled around the green extrapolated this putt to mean probable victory. How wrong we were! Andy Carter and Adrian Peacock at last justified their selection and were always in control. They eventually won by two and one after Adrian played a superb wedge shot to within four feet of the hole following Andy Carter's one hundred yard pulled hook tee shot on the seventeenth hole.

Poor Jason Osborne and Dean Roberts who had already suffered a 19th hole loss at Cherwell Edge G.C., were two up with three to play and eventually lost on the nineteenth. Their loss arising from the pressure of the situation, some excellent putts from Priors Hall and poor choices of shots from the Northampton pair. The poor guys were absolutely devastated. Golf is always a learning game, with many enjoyable and painful arrows along the way. The events that day proved to be a point of change for both players, as they subsequently reached the 2001 finals of the club's singles, foursomes and fourball competitions, a tremendous achievement.

The Northampton team consisted of mainly low handicappers at the semi–final, some higher handicap players (Paul Tee, Jamie Lloyd and Captain Gary Addington) having made a great contribution to actually getting the Club in to the semi-final. Sadly our President Tom Knight was not physically present to watch the match due to ill health. We could however feel his emotional presence being projected to the course from his hospital bed. His feeling may hopefully mend some of the emotional scares that Jason and Dean now have collected after their "Sunday Battle". This was our fourth semi-final loss in the last five attempts. I rather suspect that Tom may well have said " What a load of poof "!

Priors Hall's elation at the semi-final was unfortunately short-lived since they were thrashed five matches to nil in the final, against a heavily-fancied Peterborough Milton team, which included six current or past County players. Despite the final score it was good for the competition to see one of the less-fancied clubs challenging for the trophy. It was very sweet for the winners who ended a fifteen-year drought with a fine display of golf as favourites. Winning both the semi and final 5-0, a quite unique feat in the trophy's history. Interestingly, Jim Howkins of Kingsthorpe golf club, who played in the first final, was present at his home Club to watch the final, some forty six years later, this time he was not wearing short trousers!

Mary Bird, who is now quite a fragile lady, was present at the post match meal on the Sunday, to present the trophy to a jubilant Peterborough Milton Captain John MacCallum. This was a jewel of a weekend for their Club, as their top pair of Neil Presto & Ian Symonds retained the County Scratch Foursomes Trophy the previous day at Overstone Park.

Although this marvellous trophy has been dominated by the bigger golf Clubs, the smaller Clubs have also featured in the final. Unfortunately for those of a romantic disposition those smaller Clubs unfortunately did not quite manage to lift the trophy. Priors Hall has been the only Club to complete a hat trick of victories as a newly formed Club between 1973-5. Rushden were narrowly defeated by Peterborough in the 1976 final, when one of their players, interrupted Bill Hollingsworth's lengthy speach as he became doubled-up in agony and fell under the dinner table, since he was "crossing his legs". Oundle and Priors Hall have twice finished runners up and Cold Ashby have reached the final once. Perhaps we shall have a romantic winner in 2005 when the trophy is contested for the fiftieth time.

# THE HOLLINGSWORTH TROPHY 1956-2001

| YEAR | WINNER | *RUNNER-UP* | SCORE |
|------|--------|-------------|-------|
| 1956 | KINGSTHORPE | | |
| 1957 | DAVENTRY | OUNDLE | |
| 1958 | KINGSTHORPE | | |
| 1959 | WELLINGBOROUGH | | |
| 1960 | DAVENTRY | | |
| 1961 | KINGSTHORPE | | |
| 1962 | KINGSTHORPE | | |
| 1963 | WELLINGBOROUGH | | |
| 1964 | NORTHAMPTON | | |
| 1965 | NORTHAMPTON | | |
| 1966 | KETTERING | | |
| 1967 | KINGSTHORPE | | |
| 1968 | KETTERING | | |
| 1969 | DAVENTRY | WELLINGBOROUGH | 4-1 |
| 1970 | PRIORS HALL | | |
| 1971 | NORTHANTS COUNTY | | |
| 1972 | NORTHANTS COUNTY | NORTHAMPTON | |
| 1973 | PRIORS HALL | | |
| 1974 | PRIORS HALL | | |
| 1975 | PRIORS HALL | | |
| 1976 | PETERBOROUGH MILTON | RUSHDEN | 3-2 |
| 1977 | PETERBOROUGH MILTON | NORTHANTS COUNTY | - |
| 1978 | NORTHAMPTON | KETTERING & DAVENTRY | 3-2 & 4-1 |
| 1979 | PETERBOROUGH MILTON | KINGSTHORPE | - |
| 1980 | STAVERTON PARK | PETERBOROUGH MILTON | 3-2 |
| 1981 | PETERBOROUGH MILTON | NORTHAMPTON | 5-0 |
| 1982 | KETTERING | NORTHAMPTON | 3-2 |
| 1983 | NORTHAMPTON | PETERBOROUGH MILTON | 4-1 |
| 1984 | WELLINGBOROUGH | NORTHANTS COUNTY | 4-1 |
| 1985 | NORTHANTS COUNTY | OUNDLE | 3-2 |
| 1986 | PETERBOROUGH MILTON | KETTERING | - |
| 1987 | NORTHAMPTON | PRIORS HALL | 4-1 |

| 1988 | NORTHAMPTON | PETERBOROUGH MILTON | 3.5-1.5 |
| 1989 | KETTERING | KINGSTHORPE | 4-1 |
| 1990 | KETTERING | KINGSTHORPE | 3-2 |
| 1991 | KINGSTHORPE | KETTERING | 3-2 |
| 1992 | KETTERING | NORTHANTS COUNTY | 3-2 |
| 1993 | STAVERTON PARK | KETTERING | 3-2 |
| 1994 | NORTHANTS COUNTY | KINGSTHORPE | 4-1 |
| 1995 | KINGSTHORPE | COLD ASHBY | 4.5-0.5 |
| 1996 | NORTHAMPTON | PETERBOROUGH MILTON | 5-0 |
| 1997 | KINGSTHORPE | NORTHANTS COUNTY | 3-2 |
| 1998 | NORTHANTS COUNTY | KINGSTHORPE | 3-2 |
| 1999 | KINGSTHORPE | COLLINGTREE PARK | 3-2 |
| 2000 | KINGSTHORPE | WELLINGBOROUGH | 4-1 |
| 2001 | PETERBOROUGH MILTON | PRIORS HALL | 5-0 |

*Gary Addington receives the Hollingsworth Trophy from Bill Hollingsworth's daughter Mary Bird at Church Brampton in 1996.*

# MULTIPLE WINNERS OF THE HOLLINGSWORTH TROPHY 1956-2001

| TEAM | NUMBER | YEARS |
|---|---|---|
| KINGSTHORPE | 10 | 1956, 58, 61, 62, 67, 91, 95, 97, 1999, 2000 |
| NORTHAMPTON | 7 | 1964, 65, 78, 83, 87, 88, 1996 |
| KETTERING | 6 | 1966, 68, 82, 89, 90, 1992 |
| PETERBOROUGH | 6 | 1976, 77,79, 81, 86, 2001 |
| NORTHANTS COUNTY | 5 | 1971, 72, 85, 94, 98 |
| PRIORS HALL | 4 | 1970, 73, 74, 75 |
| DAVENTRY | 3 | 1957, 60, 1969 |
| WELLINGBOROUGH | 3 | 1959, 63, 1984 |
| STAVERTON PARK | 2 | 1980, 1993 |

*Hollingsworth Trophy winners 1996. Back row, Left to Right: J. J. Varco, J. M. Lloyd, D. A. Dare, A. J. Limbert, N. J. Frost, C. MacKenzie, S. J. Bailey, D. J. Jessup, A. J. Peacock, G. J. Riddall. Front row, Left to Right: S. P. Tootell, A. J. Carter, P. R. Huntley (Club Captain), G. P. Addington (Team Captain), M. J. Izzard, K. Heard, G. H. Keates.*

# CHAPTER 24

# Scratch League

" Imagination is more important than knowledge " Albert Einstein

THE Northamptonshire Golf Union, to provide a mechanism to evaluate current and potential County player's performances and to provide a format for competition between clubs without the use of handicaps, originally invented the Scratch League in 1980. We were along with Wellingborough G.C. the first winners of these trophies. W.P.Cross, Esq., originally presented the first division trophy as the Inter Club Challenge in 1921 before conversion to its current format. The division two trophy was presented by past County President Don Bates and Richard Seddon. The division three and four trophies were presented by the Union in 1996.

It was to be a further seven years before we once again lifted the division two trophy having spent only one year in division one. In fact this has become a frustrating though recurring theme as we have bounced back and forward between division two and one. For the record we have won the second division trophy in 1980, 1987, 1991 and in the Millennium year 2000. Perhaps in 2001 we should remain in division one!

The player's performances are now evaluated using a new scoring index, which compares player's performances between Clubs in each division. The Izzard Index is calculated using the formula below and used by the Union to assist in the selection of players:-

$$\text{Izzard Index} = \frac{\frac{\text{\% Victories} \times \text{Number of Appearances Squared}}{\text{Two} \times (1 + \text{Number of losses})}}{100}$$

In the Millenium year the following performances were achieved in the two top divisions. The top six players were: -

## Division One Millennium Winners Northants County

| Player | Club | Izzard Index |
|---|---|---|
| Neil Presto | Peterborough Milton | 16.6 |
| Jimmy Ellis | Peterborough Milton | 14.9 |
| Tony Lord | Northants County | 10.5 |
| Darren Spragg | Collingtree Park | 5.8 |
| Dave Morris | Kingsthorpe | 5.8 |
| Paul Stones | Kingsthorpe | 5.5 |

It was interesting to note that although Northants County dominated division one, the top performances in the division came from Peterborough's old and young boys. This demonstrates what a team game the scratch league is, with an eight-man team format. Poor old Dave Morris at Kingsthorpe had the best performance in the scratch league of the whole Club yet was dropped for the Hollingsworth final! He has subsequently left the Club.

## Division Two Millennium Winners Northampton

| Player | Club | Izzard Index |
|---|---|---|
| A.J.Limbert | Northampton | 12.5 |
| P.Taylor | Staverton Park | 10.1 |
| A.Tallantire | Cold Ashby | 9.6 |
| S.Hallam | Cherwell Edge | 7.4 |
| A.J.Izzard | Northampton | 7.2 |
| D.Russell | Farthingstone | 7 |

Clearly the two Northampton player's performances have helped in the team being promoted. Paul Taylor has an enviable local record, yet does not appear to have the desire or internal trust to commit himself to a more demanding County scene. Surprise package Tallantire sprung to prominence despite being off a handicap of seven, still that is match play compared to medal golf.

The Club's team produced the following statistics in 2000: -

| Player | Played | Won | Halved | Lost | Percent | Izzard Index |
|---|---|---|---|---|---|---|
| Andy Limbert | 5 | 5 | 0 | 0 | 100 | 12.5 |
| Simon Tootell | 8 | 3 | 4 | 1 | 63 | 10.1 |
| Alex Izzard | 6 | 5 | 0 | 1 | 80 | 7.2 |
| Glenn Keates | 6 | 4 | 1 | 1 | 75 | 6.8 |
| Jon Lloyd | 6 | 4 | 1 | 1 | 75 | 6.8 |
| Andy Carter | 8 | 3 | 3 | 2 | 56 | 6 |
| Jason Osborne | 4 | 1 | 3 | 0 | 63 | 5 |
| Dominic Jessup | 5 | 2 | 2 | 1 | 60 | 3.8 |
| Gavin Condon | 8 | 4 | 0 | 4 | 50 | 3.2 |
| Martin Izzard | 5 | 3 | 0 | 2 | 60 | 2.5 |
| Andrian Peacock | 2 | 0 | 1 | 1 | 25 | 0.3 |
| Alex Wray | 1 | 0 | 0 | 1 | 0 | 0 |

# RESULTS FROM THE INDIVIDUAL MATCHES

### Versus Farthingstone

| Farthingstone 4 | Northampton 4 | Northampton 5 | Farthingstone 3 |
|---|---|---|---|
| D.Matthews Halved | S.P.Tootell Halved | G.H.Keates Halved | D.Matthews Halved |
| P.Rosier 1up | A.J.Carter | S.P.Tootell 7/5 | C.Lawrence |
| D.Woolacott 5/3 | G.P.Condon | G.P.Condon | P.Rosier 2up |
| B.Jones | M.J.Izzard 2/1 | A.J.Limbert 3/1 | P.Turner |
| D.Hayle | J.M.Lloyd 2up | A.J.Carter 2/1 | D.Hayle |
| A.Pagett 3/1 | A.Peacock | A.J.Izzard 4/3 | A.Pagett |
| S.Chalcraft | A.J.Izzard 2/1 | J.Osborne Halved | B.Jones Halved |
| S.Reynolds Halved | J.Osborne Halved | A.P.Wray | D.Woolacott 5/4 |

### Versus Cherwell Edge

| Northampton 5.5 | Cherwell Edge 2.5 | Cherwell Edge 5 | Northampton 3 |
|---|---|---|---|
| S.P.Tootell Halved | C.Lowe Halved | C.Lowe 1up | S.P.Tootell |
| G.H.Keates 2/1 | K.Cole | S.Hallam 3/2 | G.H.Keates |
| D.J.Jessup Halved | J.Mumford Halved | J.Mumford 3/2 | G.P.Condon |
| A.J.Carter Halved | S.Hallam Halved | D.Newman | A.J.Carter 1up |
| G.P.Condon 6/4 | D.Newman | G.Collett 3/2 | J.M.Lloyd |
| M.J.Izzard | D.Booker 2/1 | I.Hammond | A.J.Limbert 3/2 |
| A.J.Izzard 5/3 | G.Collett | D.Booker 3/2 | M.J.Izzard |
| J.Osborne 3/2 | J.Burman | O.King | A.J.Izzard 1up |

### Versus Cold Ashby

| Northampton 5 | Cold Ashby 3 | Cold Ashby 2 | Northampton 6 |
|---|---|---|---|
| S.P.Tootell | G.Croxton 1up | G.Croxton | S.P.Tootell 4/3 |
| G.H.Keates 4/2 | A.Smith | A.Smith 4/3 | D.J.Jessup |
| D.J.Jessup Halved | M.Rigby Halved | M.Rigby | G.P.Condon 7/6 |
| A.J.Carter 4/3 | S.Young | L.Watson | A.J.Carter 2/1 |
| G.P.Condon 3/1 | S.Robertson | S.Robertson | J.M.Lloyd 3/1 |
| J.M.Lloyd Halved | L.Watson Halved | S.Hancock | A.J.Limbert 3/1 |
| A.J.Peacock Halved | M.Conway Halved | A.Tallentire | M.J.Izzard 1up |
| J.Osborne Halved | P.Askew Halved | D.Burgess 3/2 | A.J.Izzard |

### Versus Staverton Park

| Staverton Park 2 | Northampton 6 | Northampton 7 | Staverton Park 1 |
|---|---|---|---|
| P.Taylor 5/4 | G.P.Condon | G.H.Keates 4/2 | M.Franklin |
| S.Brown | G.H.Keates 5/4 | S.P.Tootell Halved | S.Harris Halved |
| D.Shandley Halved | S.P.Tootell Halved | G.P.Condon 2/1 | S.Brown |
| D.Gill | D.J.Jessup 5/4 | D.J.Jessup 1 up | M.Forgione |
| J.O'Hagen | A.J.Limbert 7/6 | J.M.Lloyd 3/2 | K.Rush |
| C.Ray Halved | A.J.Carter Halved | A.J.Limbert 7/5 | T.Sawyer |
| M.Forgione | J.M.Lloyd 2/1 | A.J.Carter Halved | S.Brennan Halved |
| S.Brennan | M.J.Izzard 3/2 | A.J.Izzard 9/7 | R.Cook |

Our performances against Staverton Park were undoubtedly the key to our success especially the away win of 6 matches to 2. Captain Gary Addington described this victory as, "This was without doubt our best Scratch League result for many years. A truly outstanding team performance, and a magnificent result for the Club. I am delighted for the players who were superb".

The final game of the season saw us thrash a weakened Staverton team where there were a few notable happenings. The combined weight in game number five was a massive thirty-five stone where our local heavyweight Jon Lloyd trimmed up his slightly heavier opponent by 3/2. In game number six Tom Sawyer was so disappointed at his performance when losing 7/5 against the level par produced by Andy Limbert, he went straight home without speaking. He was back in Daventry before the completion of the match! Young son of mine Alex "One Jab" Izzard only had to go to the eleventh green for an early bath following a 9/7 win.

Gary's comments following this 7/1 thrashing at Harlestone displays Gary's pride in his Captaincy and our Club. " On a day that meant so much to us, the players produced an excellent team performance which put Northampton Golf Club back in Division 1 for the first time since 1992. During the Scratch League campaign the going got tough at times, but every time this happened we produced some superb team golf to achieve the promotion we had failed to do for the last seven years. I cannot speak more highly of our players who have worked so hard to win us promotion in this the Millenium Golf Year, and have represented the Club with such pride and dignity. I am so proud of the team fulfilling my dream and Saturday the 22nd July 2000 will be a day I will never forget. Well done Team-you have been magnificent! We now look forward to life in division one where we shall take up the challenge especially with old and arch rivals Kingsthorpe!"

## Millenium Scratch League Final Positions Divisions 1-4

| Division 1 | Played | Won | Drawn | Lost | For | Agst | Points | Holes Won | Holes Lost |
|---|---|---|---|---|---|---|---|---|---|
| Northants County | 8 | 7 | 0 | 1 | 39.5 | 24.5 | 14 | 116 | 75 |
| Kingsthorpe | 8 | 5 | 1 | 2 | 32.5 | 31.5 | 11 | 102 | 87 |
| P'borough Milton | 8 | 3 | 1 | 4 | 31.5 | 32.5 | 7 | 92 | 93 |
| Collingtree Park | 8 | 2 | 1 | 5 | 30 | 34 | 5 | 77 | 92 |
| Kettering | 8 | 1 | 1 | 6 | 26.5 | 37.5 | 3 | 65 | 105 |

| Division 2 | Played | Won | Drawn | Lost | For | Agst | Points | Holes Won | Holes Lost |
|---|---|---|---|---|---|---|---|---|---|
| **Northampton** | **8** | **6** | **1** | **1** | **41.5** | **22.5** | **13** | **121** | **44** |
| Cherwell Edge | 8 | 4 | 2 | 2 | 33.5 | 30.5 | 10 | 93 | 78 |
| Staverton Park | 8 | 3 | 1 | 4 | 30.5 | 33.5 | 7 | 88 | 93 |
| Cold Ashby | 8 | 3 | 0 | 5 | 28.5 | 35.5 | 6 | 63 | 100 |
| Farthingstone | 8 | 0 | 4 | 4 | 26 | 38 | 4 | 48 | 98 |

| Division 3 | Played | Won | Drawn | Lost | For | Agst | Points | Holes Won | Holes Lost |
|---|---|---|---|---|---|---|---|---|---|
| Brampton Heath | 8 | 5 | 0 | 3 | 39.5 | 24.5 | 10 | 106 | 54 |
| Wellingborough | 8 | 4 | 1 | 3 | 33.5 | 30.5 | 9 | 98 | 97 |
| Rushden | 8 | 4 | 1 | 3 | 33 | 31 | 9 | 97 | 98 |
| Stoke Albany | 8 | 4 | 0 | 4 | 29 | 35 | 8 | 90 | 95 |
| Oundle | 8 | 2 | 0 | 6 | 24.5 | 39.5 | 4 | 63 | 120 |

| Division 4 | Played | Won | Drawn | Lost | For | Agst | Points | Holes Won | Holes Lost |
|---|---|---|---|---|---|---|---|---|---|
| Overstone Park | 5 | 4 | 0 | 1 | 27 | 13 | 8 | 98 | 45 |
| Hellidon Lakes | 5 | 3 | 0 | 2 | 24 | 16 | 6 | 74 | 45 |
| Daventry | 5 | 3 | 0 | 2 | 23.5 | 16.5 | 6 | 86 | 56 |
| Priors Hall | 5 | 2 | 0 | 3 | 17 | 23 | 4 | 50 | 77 |
| West Park | 5 | 2 | 0 | 3 | 14 | 26 | 4 | 56 | 94 |
| Delapre Park | 5 | 1 | 0 | 4 | 14.5 | 25.5 | 2 | 35 | 82 |

# 2001 Scratch League Division 1

Having gained promotion in the Millenium year, one could not have predicted what fireworks and emotions we were to encounter in this remarkable season. The opening game of the season was against our archrivals Kingsthorpe and what a way to start the campaign!

Playing in our first division one game since 1992 on the 27 July 2001, this closely contested match created a veritable mountain of paperwork since the result hinged on a rules decision. In the top game our player's ball was seen to finish at the bottom of a deep hole made by an old staked tree post, in a game which either finished all square or one up to Northampton. The ruling would determine if the match result was a win 4 to 3 or a halved match 4/4. As the two teams milled around the outside of the clubhouse in two separate camps we needed an accurate ruling from an unbiased source before anyone was prepared to sign the match sheet. The highly experienced County referee Roger Tippler ruled (Rule 25 Decisions 14&18) that it was in fact a free drop, giving Northampton their first win over our bogey side Kingsthorpe for 11 years.

A certain level of celebration occurred at the Club, tempered with the knowledge that we had to play Collingtree at home the following day, where we only managed a halved match. Unfortunately certain members of Kingsthorpe were not entirely happy with the decision and requested "clarification". Letters and telephone conversations flowed over the next few weeks between the Clubs, the Golf Union and the R&A, who un-surprisingly confirmed Roger's original decision. For the record the match sheets of these historic victories are given below. This away victory acted as a catalyst for a greater level of self-belief and confidence in our players, which resulted in some great team performances over the autumn of 2001.

Despite a whitewash thrashing away to Northants County, the team looked forward to tackling the old foe at Harlestone. The return leg at home was always going to have an edge to it due to the controversy the previous month. The team demolished Kingsthorpe 7/1 for long-awaited sweet revenge, which put us into contention for the title and signalled Kingsthorpe's likely demotion to division two. Although this may sound like intense rivalry some of the players have been competing against each other for over twenty years and have become good friends. It is only the behaviour of the minority of their "less agreeable players" who generate the powerful emotion of hate. This was soon followed by a superb second away win of the season at Collingtree Park, which put us top of division one for the first time ever in the history of the competition which began in 1980. After six matches we were one point ahead of the 2001 Hollingsworth Trophy winners, highly fancied Peterborough Milton who were looking to complete the double.

The second crunch match of the season loomed on the horizon for Sunday 30th September Peterborough Milton away. Where victory would probably ensure winning the league for the first time in the Club's history. A thought that no one would have superstitiously dared to consider early season, when statements such as, " Let's just try and stay up", "We have nothing to lose", were often heard in anticipation of the campaign. The match at Peterborough Milton turned out to be a totally damp squib since we lost heavily only winning two games which removed any thoughts on winning the league. Their last match of the season was at home where victory over Kingsthorpe delivered the Hollingsworth and Scratch League double. Northampton eventually finished runners up, our archrivals being demoted to division two!

### *SWEET SUCCESS OVER OUR ARCHRIVALS 2001*

### SCRATCH LEAGUE DIVISION 1
### 27 JULY 2001 AT KINGSTHORPE

#### KINGSTHORPE 3    NORTHAMPTON 4

| PLAYER | HCP | RESULT | PLAYER | HCP | SCORE |
|--------|-----|--------|--------|-----|-------|
| J.EVANS | SCR | HALVED | G.H.KEATES | +1 | HALVED |
| P.STONES | 2 | WON | S.P.TOOTELL | 1 | 5/4 |
| G.THOMAS | 2 | HALVED | D.J.JESSUP | 1 | HALVED |
| S.CROWSON | 3 | LOST | G.P.CONDON | 1 | 4/3 |
| P.SCOTT | 4 | WON | J.M.LLOYD | 2 | 1 UP |
| J.WALDING | 5 | LOST | A.J.LIMBERT | 3 | 2/1 |
| S.BLUNDELL | 5 | LOST | A.J.CARTER | 3 | 1UP |
| D.ROBERTS | 5 | HALVED | M.J.IZZARD | 4 | HALVED |

## SCRATCH LEAGUE DIVISION 1
## 25 AUGUST 2001 AT HARLESTONE

### NORTHAMPTON 7     KINGSTHORPE 1

| PLAYER | HCP | RESULT | PLAYER | HCP | SCORE |
|---|---|---|---|---|---|
| G.H.KEATES | +1 | WON | J.EVANS | SCR | 1UP |
| S.P.TOOTELL | 1 | WON | S.CROWSON | 3 | 4/3 |
| D.J.JESSUP | 1 | LOST | P.CROXFORD | 4 | 4/3 |
| J.M.LLOYD | 2 | WON | P.SCOTT | 4 | 3/2 |
| A.J.CARTER | 4 | WON | S.McDONALD | 4 | 5/4 |
| A.J.IZZARD | 4 | WON | D.ROBERTS | 5 | 2 UP |
| M.J.IZZARD | 4 | WON | M.BAZELEY | 5 | 2/1 |
| A.J.PEACOCK | 5 | WON | P.HARRIS | 5 | 1 UP |

*Millennium Scratch League, Division Two Winners. Back row, Left to Right: D. J. Jessup, A. J. Carter, A. J. Izzard, G. Condon, J. M. Lloyd, A. J. Limbert, A. J. Peacock, J. Osborne. Front row, Left to Right: M. J. Izzard, G. H. Keates, T. C. A. Knight (President), G. P. Addington (Captain), A. R. G. Harrison (Club Captain), S. P. Tootell, A. P. Wray.*

# CHAPTER 25

# Dazeley Trophies

"Golf is the most fun I've ever had with my clothes on"

Lee Trevino

**PRESENTED by Mr. George Dazeley Jun in remembrance of his mother and father's association with the Club. Presented in 1965, this trophy is played as a mixed foursome knockout competition during the summer months. Handicap limits Gentlemen 20, Ladies 27.**

This surely must be the ultimate challenge in golf, handicap foursomes often played with the wife! I bet there are many detailed inquests carried out after such a game, which must tax the nerves to the limit. One wonders how often the male part of the partnership has cooked his own tea the following day! To be quite fair in this age of equality, husband and wife pairs have won this competition thirteen times from a possible thirty-two starts.

Many successful pairings have been produced over the years. The most successful pairing are Nick and Peggy Durant who have won the trophies on four occasions in 1969,71,75 and 1980. The trophies have been retained twice by Paul and Carol Oakenfull in 1977 and by Neil Frost and Vera White in 1997.

Jean Douglas and Keith Heard could possibly be accused of being "partner pickers", since they have been winners three times and twice respectively each time with a different partner.

The Millenium winners were Charles and Joan Peacock, adding this title to a growing list of mixed titles at Club and County level.

| | | | |
|---|---|---|---|
| 1965 | M.S.FLOYD | 1989 | I.R.FARMER |
| | Miss J.DOUGLAS | | Mrs I.R.FARMER |
| 1966 | H.MILNER | 1990 | P.L.BEEBY |
| | Mrs R.V.TRIGG | | Mrs J.MacKENZIE |

| | | | |
|---|---|---|---|
| 1967 | C.C.WESTON | 1991 | J.HALLWOOD |
| | Mrs C.WESTON | | Mrs P.HALLWOOD |
| 1968 | H.G.BROWN | 1992 | R.T.F.WILLOUGHBY |
| | Mrs R.HALLIDAY | | Mrs C.A.OAKENFULL |
| 1969 | N.C.DURANT | 1993 | B.J.OLLIVE |
| | Mrs C.DURANT | | Mrs P.L.OLLIVE |
| 1970 | F.MASSON | 1994 | M.BLAKE |
| | Mrs J.R.TONG | | Mrs N.BLAKE |
| 1971 | N.C.DURANT | 1995 | D.COOMBES |
| | Mrs C.DURANT | | Miss L.SHERRY |
| 1972 | H.MILMER | 1996 | N.FROST |
| | Miss J.DOUGLAS | | Mrs.V.WHITE |
| 1973 | A.F.STEVENS | 1997 | N.FROST |
| | MISS J.DOUGLAS | | MRS.V.WHITE |
| 1974 | A.F.STEVENS | 1998 | Mrs. A.SPAVEN |
| | MISS J.SANDERS | | Mr.A.WEST |
| 1975 | N.C.DURANT | 1999 | Mr.K.HEARD |
| | Mrs C.DURANT | | Mrs.M.FROST |
| 1976 | P.C.OAKENFULL | 2000 | Mr&Mrs C.G.PEACOCK |
| | Mrs P.C.OAKENFULL | | |
| 1977 | P.C.OAKENFULL | 2001 | Mr.B.PAGE |
| | Mrs P.C.OAKENFULL | | Mrs.C.PAGE |
| 1978 | A.J.PARKER | 2002 | |
| | Mrs A.J.PARKER | | |
| 1979 | A.PANTER | 2003 | |
| | Mrs A.PANTER | | |
| 1980 | N.C.DURANT | 2004 | |
| | Mrs C.DURANT | | |
| 1981 | J.A.SALE | 2005 | |
| | Mrs E.H.TRAHEARN | | |
| 1982 | R.W.WHITTAKER | 2006 | |
| | Mrs E.BARKER | | |
| 1983 | R.RAGBIR | 2007 | |
| | Miss S.EVERARD | | |
| 1984 | R.J.C.KILLIP | 2008 | |
| | Mrs F.STORR | | |
| 1985 | A.STILL | 2009 | |
| | Mrs N.RUSSELL | | |
| 1986 | P.McKENZIE | 2010 | |
| | Mrs P.McKENZIE | | |
| 1987 | B.J.STANBRIDGE | 2011 | |
| | Mrs C.E.STANBRIDGE | | |
| 1988 | K.HEARD | 2012 | |
| | Miss S.CARTER 3/2 | | |

# CHAPTER 26

# Vaughan Morris

"If you think it's hard to meet new people, try picking up the wrong golf ball"

Jack Lemmon

**VAUGHAN was a very flamboyant character who used to encourage the Junior golfers despite an age gap of some forty-odd years. He was always interested in their scores and if they had enjoyed themselves. My nickname as a seventeen-year-old was Cherokee, which Vaughan decided due to my Indian-like appearance of a red headband and shoulder length hair. I used to sport this image prior to the tennis brat John McEnroe. There are a few current Club members with long memories, who might argue that the author similarly displayed these emotions and behaviour at the time. I could not possibly comment!**

The most successful male in this competition has been David Dare who has been victorious over three decades in 1984,1996 and 2001, each time with a different partner. Peggy Durant, again, is the most prolific Lady winner with three titles to her name in 1983,1984 and 1994. In the 1990's the Craddock's have their name recorded three times, there is still time for Richard to catch up!

| | | | |
|---|---|---|---|
| 1979 | Mr.J.HADDON | 1995 | Mr.I.BILLSON |
| | Mrs E.PARKER | | Mrs.J.CRADDOCK |
| 1980 | Mr.H.E.RICHARDS | 1996 | Mr.D.A.DARE |
| | Mrs.E.BARKER | | Mrs.B.DUNN |
| 1981 | Mr.R.A.SIMPSON | 1997 | Mr.J.C.W.STEELE |
| | Mrs.P.C.OAKENFULL | | Mrs.G.COOPER |

| | | | |
|---|---|---|---|
| 1982 | Mr.P.M.BARRETT | 1998 | Mr.R.COLEMAN |
| | Mrs.J.McKENZIE | | Mrs.S.AVISON |
| 1983 | Mr.R.RAGBIR | 1999 | Mr.R.E.CRADDOCK |
| | Mrs.P.DURANT | | Mrs.E.WILMER |
| 1984 | Mr.D.DARE | 2000 | Mr.R.COLEMAN |
| | Mrs.P. DURANT | | Mrs.V.WHITE |
| 1985 | Mr.D.A.DARE | 2001 | Mr.D.DARE |
| | Mrs.F.STORR | | Mrs.M.NUTT    38pts |
| 1986 | Mr.K.BROWNLESS | 2002 | |
| | Mrs.J.FELL | | |
| 1987 | Mr.B.J.FROST | 2003 | |
| | Mrs.S.PEARSON | | |
| 1988 | Mr.A.J.PARKER | 2004 | |
| | Mrs.J.FARMER | | |
| 1989 | Mr.B.J.STANBRIDGE | 2005 | |
| | Mrs.S.PEARSON | | |
| 1990 | Mr.J.HALLWOOD | 2006 | |
| | Mrs.J.CALVERT | | |
| 1991 | Mr.D.A.DARE | 2007 | |
| | Mrs.B.HARRIS | | |
| 1992 | Mr.S.J.PARKER | 2008 | |
| | Mrs.J.CRADDOCK | | |
| 1993 | Mr.R.WHITTACKER | 2009 | |
| | Mrs.A.ARMITAGE | | |
| 1994 | Mr.B.OLLIVE | 2010 | |
| | Mrs.P.DURANT | | |

# CHAPTER 27

# Silver Salvers

" You make a lot of money at this game. Just ask my ex-wives. Both of them are so rich that neither of their husbands work ".

Lee Trevino

**MR.AUBREY WATSON presented the trophy to the Club in 1934. The Club bought a second Salver so that the winning side might each hold a trophy for one year. The competition is played under Medal rules as Foursomes (Mixed) the maximum handicaps being Gentlemen 20, Ladies 27.**

This competition is the oldest of the Mixed competitions now in its sixty sixth year. It was not until 1964 that a husband and wife combination lifted the trophy, which was retained the following year by Richard and Janet Halliday. Since that time husband and wife combinations have been quite successful to date.

The most unusual combination to have won the Salvers was perhaps County golfer Alan Linney and Ladies' stalwart Dilys Tyrrell in 1987. Some wags have suggested that Alan only played because he was allowed to borrow a hairdryer after the game! I could not possibly comment. Past Captains Ben and Maureen Middleton were victorious in 1998.

During the nineteen nineties the Salvers were won a remarkable three times from four starts by Keith and Helen Brownless, Barry and Christine Stanbridge preventing a clean sweep in 1991.

James Hallwood and Pat Dare won the 2001 competition with a score of 71. Martin & Sue Harris actually scored a superb nett 62 from the wrong tees and were disqualified! The reason why they played from the yellow tees was poor information from one of our gentleman members with a lady's nickname. The Harris's were justifiably distraught, though philo-sophical about milking the situation in the future.

| 1935 | Mrs E.CAPLIN | 1977 | A.J.PARKER |
|------|--------------|------|------------|
| | G.MARKIE 76 Nett | | Mrs A.J.PARKER 69 |
| 1936 | Mrs W.T.SWANNELL | 1978 | H.G.BROWN |
| | C.S.CATLOW 75 | | Mrs H.G.BROWN 68 |
| 1937 | Mrs B.J.JELLEYMAN | 1979 | J.A.GRAHAM |
| | R.S.JELLYMAN 69 | | Mrs A.MEADOWS |
| 1938 | Miss C.R.BUCKANAN | 1980 | K.BILLINGHAM |
| | F.C.ROE 74 | | Mrs E.COOK |
| 1939 | Miss E.R.SPACKMAN | 1981 | C.DURANT |
| | F.ALIBONE 71 | | Mrs E.KING |
| 1940-44 | WORLD WAR 2 | 1982 | R.C.PRIOR |
| | | | Mrs J.PRIOR |
| 1945 | Miss M.HOLLINGSWORTH | 1983 | N.C.DURANT |
| | H.C.ANDERSON 69 1/2 | | Mrs P.DURANT |
| 1946 | Mrs H.E.LACEY | 1984 | R.G.BUSWELL |
| | W.H.ABBOTT 73 1/2 | | Miss J.GOLDEN |
| 1947 | Mrs G.E.DAZELEY | 1985 | A.J.PARKER |
| | W.H.CHAPMAN | | Mrs A.J.PARKER |
| 1948 | Miss S.F.GREIG | 1986 | J.T.HADDON |
| | A.J.HARRISON | | Mrs E.BARBER |
| 1949 | Mrs C.C.WESTON | 1987 | A.J.LINNEY |
| | G.F.CLARKE | | Mrs D.E.TYRRELL |
| 1950 | Mrs C.C.WESTON | 1988 | P.McKENZIE |
| | G.F.CLARKE | | Mrs P.McKENZIE |
| 1951 | Miss F.BROWN | 1989 | K.G.BROWNLESS |
| | W.K.HUNTER | | Mrs K.G.BROWNLESS |
| 1952 | Mrs R.W.CLARKE | 1990 | K.G.BROWNLESS |
| | R.W.CLARKE | | Mrs K.G.BROWNLESS |
| 1953 | Mrs R.S.MUMFORD | 1991 | B.J.STANBRIDGE |
| | R.L.CLARKE | | Mrs B.J.STANBRIDGE |
| 1954 | Mrs C.C.WESTON | 1992 | K.G.BROWNLESS |
| | D.C.SOUTHEY 71 | | Mrs K.G.BROWNLESS |
| 1955 | Mrs B.A.MARBROOK | 1993 | J.T.HADDON |
| | B.A.MARBROOK 72 | | Mrs E.BARBER |
| 1956 | Mrs M.D.COLBOURNE | 1994 | J.T.HADDON |
| | S.PANTHER 71 | | Mrs E.BARBER |
| 1957 | Mrs M.HOLLINGSWORTH | 1995 | B.RUSSELL |
| | R.C.PARTINGTON 71 | | Mrs C.RUSSELL |
| 1958 | Mrs E.NEEDHAM | 1996 | P.TAYLOR |
| | F.BONHAM 69 | | Mrs A.TAYLOR |
| 1959 | Miss M.PEARSON | 1997 | K.BROWNLESS |
| | F.G.RIDDICK 69 | | MRS V.WHITE |
| 1960 | Mrs COLBOURNE | 1998 | Mr B.MIDDLETON |
| | D.C.SOUTHEY 69 | | Mrs B.MIDDLETON |

| | | | |
|---|---|---|---|
| 1961 | Mrs W.H.CHAPMAN<br>W.H.CHAPMAN 67 | 1999 | Mr & Mrs B.L.ARMITAGE |
| 1962 | Miss L.HARRY<br>W.DEMPSEY 68 | 2000 | Mr.D.GORE<br>Miss M.MOTTRAM |
| 1963 | F.E.DOUGLAS<br>Mrs E.C.KOTTLER 70 | 2001 | Mr. J.HALLWOOD<br>Mrs. P.DARE 71 |
| 1964 | Mr & Mrs R.G.HALLIDAY 63 | 2002 | |
| 1965 | Mrs R.HALLIDAY<br>R.G.HALLIDAY 70 | 2003 | |
| 1966 | Mrs C.WESTON<br>C.C.WESTON 72 | 2004 | |
| 1967 | F.E.DOUGLAS<br>Mrs R.A.TAYLOR 68 | 2005 | |
| 1968 | G.B.PYKE<br>Mrs R.BIRD 75 | 2006 | |
| 1969 | D.ABEL<br>Miss L.HARRY 69 | 2007 | |
| 1970 | J.HURLEY<br>Mrs J.HURLEY 70 | 2008 | |
| 1971 | D.ABEL<br>Miss L.HARRY 67 | 2009 | |
| 1972 | B.PICKERELL<br>Mrs B.PICKERELL 68 | 2010 | |
| 1973 | D.ABEL<br>Miss L.HARRY 69 | 2011 | |
| 1974 | J.TRAHEARN<br>Mrs B.TRAHEARN 71 | 2012 | |
| 1975 | R.M.BUCHAN<br>Mrs R.BUCHAN 74 | | |
| 1976 | J.HALLIWELL<br>Mrs R.S.PAGE 67 | | |

*The demanding tee shot to the sixteenth hole at Harlestone.*

# CHAPTER 28

# Trahearn Trophy

"I know you understand what you think I have said but I am not so sure that what you heard is what I meant".

Anon

**PRIOR to this competition being known as the Trahearn trophy it was played for as the family foursomes since 1961 as a nett competition off handicap. This trophy was originally presented by the family in 1972 in memory of Arthur (Trigger) Trahearn initially and then remembered in later years for Beth Trahearn, who was a feisty character at the Club with a solid heart. Beth always knew what she wanted!**

Their son, James (J.W.H.) Trahearn, was a fine player and played in several County trials at the old course. He moved away to become a member of that wonderful Nottinghamshire Club Hollinwell and became their Treasurer. Hollinwell is one of the most beautiful inland courses in England. When the Trahearn Trophy is played for in June it has a lovely pink hue. The rough is locally called the pink, since the local flora, which is allowed to grow to eighteen inches long, is coloured peachy pink. It would be appropriate for James to come back to the Club and present the family trophy on its thirtieth anniversary in 2002. Male/male combinations have slightly dominated this competition, where the father/son combination has secured the trophy fifteen times. The husband /wife combination has featured relatively well through the years. Only one Miss has settled on the winning podium, Kelly Hanwell allegedly carrying her father to victory in 1992. Kelly has in the last few years been in the U.S.A. on a golf scholarship at Arkansas University and we have only seen her on home visits. We shall have to look out in this competition on her return. David and Patricia Dare finally joined their hands together on the trophy in 1997, having been runners up on four occasions.

The day's play is started at lunchtime and followed by a meal where all caddies and players sit down together prior to the presentation. The trophy is only presented on the day.

| 1961 | W.BOTWOOD |
| | R.BOTWOOD 65 |
| 1962 | Mr.C.WESTON |
| | Mrs.WESTON 70 |
| 1963 | W.PETTIGREW |
| | J.PETTIGREW 74 |
| 1964 | J.S. DAVIDSON |
| | G.J.DAVIDSON 66 1/2 |
| 1965 | C.R.CEISLEWICZ |
| | J.T.CEISLEWICZ 71 1/2 |
| 1966 | Mr.R.TONG |
| | Mrs.TONG 65 |
| 1967 | D.MACE |
| | G.MACE 69 |
| 1968 | Mr.R.BUCHAN |
| | Mrs.R.BUCHAN 72 |
| 1969 | Mr.S.J.COOK |
| | Mr.T.COOK 68 |
| 1970 | Mr.R.V.TRIGG |
| | Mrs.TRIGG 67 1/2 |
| 1971 | R.KNEWMAN |
| | K.NEWMAN 61 |
| 1972 | **NOW TRAHEARN FF** |
| | W.G.BOTWOOD |
| | R.S.BOTWOOD 65 Nett |
| 1973 | R.V.TRIGG |
| | Mrs R.V.TRIGG 72 |
| 1974 | R.A.WATSON |
| | A.A.WATSON 68 1/2 |
| 1975 | B.D.J.PICKERELL |
| | Mrs B.PICKERELL 65 |
| 1976 | M.BURNHOPE |
| | D.BURNHOPE 67 |
| 1977 | C.P.PAINTON |
| | M.PAINTON 67 |
| 1978 | R.NEWMAN |
| | K.NEWMAN 70 |
| 1979 | J.A.KELLY |
| | S.KELLEY |
| 1980 | R.NEWMAN |
| | J.UNDERWOOD |

| 1981 | B.J.MEADOWS |
| | A.G.MEADOWS |
| 1982 | D.C.PRIOR |
| | R.C.PRIOR |
| 1983 | B.J.OLLIVE |
| | Mrs.B.OLLIVE |
| 1984 | P.McKENZIE |
| | Mrs.P. McKENZIE |
| 1985 | R.W.RIDDALL |
| | G.RIDDALL |
| 1986 | C.G.PEACOCK |
| | A.J.PEACOCK |
| 1987 | K.CALVERT |
| | Mrs. J.CALVERT |
| 1988 | M.NEWMAN |
| | Mrs.S.NEWMAN |
| 1989 | Mr.B.J.STANBRIDGE |
| | Mrs.B.J.STANBRIDGE |
| 1990 | J.HALLWOOD |
| | Mrs.J.HALLWOOD |
| 1991 | M.HARRIS |
| | R.HARRIS 36 pts |
| 1992 | N.S.HANWELL |
| | Miss.K.HANWELL |
| | |
| 1993 | K.G.BROWNLESS |
| | Mrs.K.G.BROWNLESS |
| 1994 | K.VALLANCE |
| | S.VALLANCE |
| 1995 | P.HEATH |
| | M.HEATH |
| 1996 | Mr.M.J.IZZARD |
| | Master A.J.IZZARD 37 pts |
| 1997 | D.A.DARE |
| | Mrs.P.C.DARE |
| 1998 | R.TOOTELL |
| | S.P.TOOTELL |
| 1999 | Mr.P.HEATH |
| | Mr.M.HEATH |
| 2000 | Mr.M.J.IZZARD |
| | Mr.A.J.IZZARD 39 pts |
| 2001 | Mr.W.SHOEBRIDGE |
| | Mrs.P.SHOEBRIDGE |

*Simon and Ray Tootell, Trahearn Family Foursomes 1998.*

*Harlestone snow scenes Jan 2001 – No play today!*

# CHAPTER 29

# Ollive Bowls

"As you walk down the fairway of life you must smell the roses, for you only get to play one round"

Ben Hogan

**BRIAN OLLIVE, Captain in 1991, was a very respected Junior Organiser. Many of his juniors are stalwarts of the Club today. Paula set this trophy up in his honour. Brian's ashes were scattered on the 15th hole.**

He is well remembered throughout the playing season and especially on what is always an emotional evening when the trophies are presented. Mrs Jean Calvert is the partner every gentleman is looking for, since she has been victorious on three occasions.

| YEAR | WINNERS |
|------|---------|
| 1996 | MR.D.DARE & MRS.S.AVISON |
| 1997 | MR.D.LAIRD & MRS.J.CALVERT |
| 1998 | MR.S.HUBBLE & MRS.J.CALVERT |
| 1999 | MR.W.J.SHOEBRIDGE & MRS.J.COOPER |
| 2000 | MR.R.L.JONES & MRS.J.CALVERT |
| 2001 | MR.J.HARWOOD & MRS.S.FIELD |

*N.G.U. President T. Haley presents past Club members and County stalwarts R.G. Aitken and R.G. Halliday with a suitable memento to celebrate 40 consecutive appearances each at the 2000 County Championship.*

# CHAPTER 30

# Senior Golf at Harlestone

## by Jack Bird

"The older you get the stronger the wind gets and it's always in your face"

Jack Nicklaus

IN October 1990 we moved to our new course located at Harlestone with mixed feelings for some members. Mainly because of the extra distance some would have to travel. For myself, I was delighted because it was rather like coming home. Approximately seventy years ago, when living at New Duston, much of my childhood was spent around this lovely site at Harlestone. My friends and I were able to camp, fish, explore the woods and on quite a few occasions were able to skate on the lake. What wonderful memories.

Back at the present times, the Senior members soon adapted to the new course and its extra length with the new challenges it presented. We found the club house and its amenities quite impressive and particularly the views over the lake. Visitors to the Club were also very impressed, so it was not too difficult to obtain new venues for the Senior team matches. The later additions to the list were Buckingham, West Park, Kilworth Springs, Kibworth and Stoke Albany. These new fixtures brought the total of Clubs we are playing to sixteen, quite a formidable list when you consider they are home and away. All the new matches created a great deal of interest among Senior members and with more and more reaching retirement age we were not short of players.

Since October 1976 Northampton Golf Club has been a member of the Mid-Northants Veterans Association. In October 1998, a Captain's meeting was held at Kingsthorpe Golf Club. A majority then decided that there was little purpose in keeping the Association, so it was dissolved.

The Association had always insisted that Senior players should have a minimum age of sixty. However as this did not now apply, we reduced the minimum age to fifty five. This of course meant that even more players were eligible to play in the Seniors team events. For many years the six Clubs in the association had played annually for the Queen Elizabeth Silver Jubilee Cup. This had been donated many years ago by Maurice Jaffa of Northampton Golf Club. As it was no longer required, I brought the cup back to Harlestone where it was refurbished and it is now called the Jaffa Cup. Thank you, Maurice.

Around twelve years ago I started an annual Seniors/Wives dinner and dance. This has become very popular and is always very well-attended. Long may it continue. The course has improved enormously since we moved in and continues to do so. Our thanks go to all who have made this possible. Some years ago we started a Seniors invitation day, inviting the Clubs we play with to send teams of ten players to compete. A meal was, of course, included in the price, as were some very nice prizes, with our own players competing in a separate competition. This proved very popular, with a great number entering the competition. In fact quite a few Clubs followed suit.

The year 2000 arrived and so did my 80th birthday and I thought it was time that I found someone to take over the organization of the Seniors team. The last fifteen years have been quite wonderful. To see the Seniors team come on from practically nothing to their very strong position today is very encouraging. They really have come on from strength to strength and I have enjoyed being involved with such good sportsmen and their excellent company. During the years I have had the privilege of meeting many very nice people. I wish I could remember all their names, because so many seem to remember mine.

I would like to thank all the people who have helped in the past, not of course forgetting my dear wife who helped me such a lot. Finally, I did find someone suitable to take over the organisation and sometimes hard work of running the Seniors. This was, of course, David Prior an experienced person, ex Club Captain, a good golfer and a very nice man.

Good luck David.

*Jack Nicklaus, the best player and sportsman golf has seen to date. St. Andrews 2000.*

# CHAPTER 31

# Ladies Golf

## by Rose Heath

"Golf acts as a corrective against sinful pride. If Cleopatra had been ousted in the first round of the Ladies' Singles, we should have heard a lot less of her proud imperiousness".

P.G.Wodehouse

**THE Ladies at Northampton have always been involved in competitive golf with notable success. As well as playing in the Club's internal competitions they have been very active in County and some National competitions.**

Two of our most successful golfers of recent years have come up through our Junior ranks. Kelly Hanwell joined the Club as a Junior in 1990. She later won a scholarship to study in the U.S.A. where she played competitive college golf. Since her return in 2001 she has become Midland Ladies Champion. With her handicap now down to two she has had a very good season, breaking our course record twice. She played for England Girls in 1996. It is surely only a matter of time before the England selectors notice her. It goes without saying that she is a key member of the Northamptonshire Ladies' Team.

Sarah Carter joined the Club as a Junior in the 1980's. She has been Lady County Champion in 1996,1997 and again in 2001. She has been very active in Club competitions and she plays for the County Team.

Northampton has had many ladies who have held the title of Lady County Champion. Before Sarah there was Mrs. J.H. Paton in 1965, Mrs. G.Hollingsworth in 1961 and 1962, Mrs. J.W.Taylor in 1950 and Miss A.M. Troup in 1947 and 1949. In the focus of this book, Sarah has been our only winner.

Our ladies have had a very successful Scratch League team of recent years, the winning Shield was presented by Mrs Judy Ray in 1991. They have won this prestigious County Trophy in 1992 when the final was against Oundle G.C.; 1994 when their opponents in the final were Wellingborough G.C.; 1996 when they again met Wellingborough in the final; 1997 when they beat Northants County in the final and 1998 when they met Wellingborough once again in the final. The team also reached the semi-final stage in 1993, 1999 and 2000. This Scratch League is played in teams of three and many of the Club stalwarts of competitive golf have played in the team over recent years. To name but a few there has been Vera White (an ex Lady County Captain), Sarah Carter, Kelly Hanwell, Paula Hallwood, Jean McKenzie, Aileen Armitage, Carole Oakenfull, Rae Smith, Sue Avison, Chris Stanbridge, Linda Sherry and Jane Petts. According to the Northamptonshire Golf Union's website at http://www.ngu.org.uk only Northampton and Northants County have won this trophy to date.

Arguably the most prestigious, competition run by the Northants Ladies Golf Association (N.L.G.A.) is the Cecil Leitch competition. Ladies whose handicaps are between 12 and 35 currently play for this in a team of 7 players. Cecil Leitch (1891-1977) was a famous lady amateur golfer in the early part of the last century. She won the French Ladies five times 1912-14-20-21-24, the English Ladies' twice in 1914 &1920, the British Ladies' four times 1914-20-21-26 and the Canadian Ladies' in 1921. In the final of the Canadian Ladies' she recorded the biggest margin in a major title winning by 17 up with 15 to play. Her total of four victories in the British Ladies' has never been beaten and only equalled once by Joyce Wethered. Miss Leitch was an outspoken person who occasionally battled with the golfing authorities. Her strong attacking play mirrored her personality. Right to the end of her life in 1997, Cecil Leitch took an active interest in golf, attending major events whenever possible.

Cecil had a warm affection for this County as she had a close relative living near to Church Brampton and she often played the course there. In 1926 she gave the Cecil Leitch trophy to that Club and the Brampton Ladies' committee were asked to draw up the rules, which Cecil agreed. We were one of the original six clubs to play in this knock out competition. In 1930 a draw was held for the first time as more than 6 clubs competed and in 1934 the N.L.G.A. took over the running of the competition. Over recent years more divisions have been drawn up as more clubs in the County wish to compete, a semi-final and final stage is now necessary.

In the early years Northampton Golf Club were successful playing in the final match in the following years;

1927 Losers, 1929 Losers
1933, 34, 35, 36, 37, 47, 50, 52 Winners
1958 Losers, 1960 Winners, 1964 Losers,
1965, 1968 Winners

After 20 years in the doldrums Northampton reached the semi-final in 1999 where they lost and the year 2000 saw them losing in the final to Kettering. In 2000 Northampton fielded the same team in both the final and semi-final, consisting of Aileen Armitage, Teresa East, Olly Hickman, Mairi Young, Chris Beeby, Margaret Mottram and Sheila Field.

The final was played at Wellingborough G.C. on the 26th September 2000. We lost to Kettering 5-2. It was very close with three matches going to the 18th hole. This was Kettering's fourth consecutive final and they had been runners up for three years so perhaps they deserved to win.

Our Club also play a long-standing competition with Rugby Golf Club. This is called the Turner Cup. Two sisters presented it in 1965. One sister played at Northampton and the other at Rugby. The vets of both Clubs play a foursomes competition for this cup annually, alternating venues. As I write Northampton are the holders.

On a much more recent note, Rose Heath the 2001 Lady Captain of Northampton and Fran Wood, the 2001 Lady Captain of Wellingborough presented a plate "in friendship", as the two ladies are friends. The Clubs will compete for this when they play their annual friendly match. In 2001 Wellingborough, were the winners by a close margin.

Both weekday ladies and the Sunday or Alternate Day ladies have many friendly matches during a season all against local Clubs.

Being a Club of such history we have many prestigious cups to play for. Our main events are our Club Championship which is played off scratch and the Northampton Cup which is played off handicap. To qualify for the Northampton Cup you need to have won a medal in your division during the previous year. Both these events are played over 36 holes and are keenly contested. A list of winners in recent years is given on page 142.

There are many other competitions all displayed on the boards around the Club. Many of these go back many years. It may well be worth mentioning the Granny Vase, donated by Mrs. Mary Harrington, who was Lady Captain in 1987, is one of the most prized. This is a Stableford competition that can only be entered if you are a granny. It is surprising how hard you yearn for your grandchildren.

The Ladies section has amongst its members many stalwarts. Peggy Durant who is still a playing member after more than 60 years membership was Lady Captain in 1972, alongside her husband Charles who was men's Captain in the same year. Dilys Tyrrell is another lady member who has been in the Club for many years. She has held many offices and has recently retired as a Trustee of the Club. Like Peggy she still plays a very active part in the running of the Club. Along with other lady members these two have a wealth of stories to tell. They both remember being on bunker duty in the war when the green staff were fighting and everyone had to do their bit. Dilys can also remember being reprimanded by Peggy's father for playing golf, in a natty pair of trousers, instead of the usual skirt!

I add these anecdotes, as the competitive scene would not happen if we did not have ladies willing to support the Club and provide the framework for our successful lady golfers. Long may we continue to be successful.

| Year | Ladies Cup | Year | Ladies Cup |
|------|------------|------|------------|
| 1969 | Mrs.R.W.Clarke | 1985 | Mrs.C.Stanbridge |
| 1970 | Mrs.C.Durant | 1986 | Mrs.A.M.Black |
| 1971 | Mrs.I.Harris | 1987 | Mrs.A.M.Meadows |
| 1972 | Mrs.G.L.J.Kennedy | 1988 | Dr.M.Gill |
| 1973 | Mrs.G.Wild | 1989 | Mrs.P.Ollive |
| 1974 | Mrs.I.Harris | 1990 | Mrs.P.Hallwood |
| 1975 | Mrs.O.Wells | 1991 | Mrs.G.Cooper |
| 1976 | Mrs.M.Robertson | 1992 | Mrs.V.White |
| 1977 | Mrs.C.P.Oakenfull | 1993 | Mrs.A.Harrison |
| 1978 | Mrs.C.P.Oakenfull | 1994 | Miss.S.Carter |
| 1979 | Mrs.B.J.Meadows | 1995 | Mrs.L.Inwood |
| 1980 | Mrs.B.J.Meadows | 1996 | Mrs.J.Petts |
| 1981 | Mrs.B.J.Meadows | 1997 | Mrs.A.Armitage |
| 1982 | Mrs.J.Jones | 1998 | Mrs.V.White |
| 1983 | Mrs.P.Woods | 1999 | Mrs.C.Beeby |
| 1984 | Mrs.H.Brownless | 2000 | Miss.A.Goodchild |
|      |            | 2001 | Mrs.L.Carter |

| Year | Club Championship | Granny Vase Winners |
|------|-------------------|---------------------|
| 1987 |                   | Mrs.M.E.MacLagan |
| 1988 |                   | Mrs.D.Pickerell |
| 1989 |                   | Mrs.S.Crystal |
| 1990 |                   | Mrs.M.Crook |
| 1991 |                   | Mrs.G.Brown |
| 1992 | Mrs.V.White       | Mrs.M.E.MacLagan |
| 1993 | Mrs.P.C.Oakenfull | Mrs.M.I.Harrington |
| 1994 | Miss.S.Carter     | Mrs.J.Bowring |
| 1995 | Miss.S.Carter     | Mrs.M.Rock |
| 1996 | Miss.K.M.Hanwell  | Mrs.J.Craddock |
| 1997 | Miss.K.M.Hanwell  | Mrs.B.Harris |
| 1998 | Miss.K.M.Hanwell  | Mrs.B.Dunn |
| 1999 | Mrs.V.White       | Mrs.P.Buller |
| 2000 | Miss.S.Carter     | Mrs.N.Blake |
| 2001 | Miss.K.M.Hanwell  | Mrs.J.Fell |

"LOST: GOLFING HUSBAND AND DOG-last seen at Ratliff Ranch Golf
Links.
Reward for Dog"

Ad Section Texas Reporter 1997

*Cecil Leitch Runners up 2000.Lady Captain C.Russell, C.Black, L.Wilmer, L.Carter, Organiser
J.Keates, J.Dunn, J.Peacock, J.Turner, J.Woods.
Finalists O.Hickman, S.Field, T.East, M.Mottram, A.Armitage, C.Beeby, M.Young.*

*County Family Foursomes 2000. Runners up Mark and Peter Heath (above),*
*David and Pat Dare third (below) with N.G.U. Vice President Brian Woodcock.*

# CHAPTER 32

# Junior Golf

"In Africa some of the native tribes have a custom of beating the ground with clubs and uttering spine chilling cries. Anthropologists call this a form of self-expression. In America we call it golf"

Becker

**THE Junior scene has been very good at the Club as a breeding ground for golfers and gentlemen. We have over the last thirty years produced an impressive list of trophy winners, administrators and many new players for the Club's Hollingsworth and Scratch league teams. The "role of honour" is described in detail at the end of this chapter.**

For example, Conrad Ceislewicz became an English Boy International in 1972 and played along side the likes of Sandy Lyle and Ian Woosnam. Conrad is still felt in the hearts of young lads of that time, such as Glenn Cottrell, the author and Chris Westall, since we miss him as a friend and gentleman on the golfing scene. Conrad was County Champion five times between 1973-1980 including a hat trick of victories from 1978-1980. Conrad became County Captain in 1981, where he was forced to deal with certain difficult situations to which he was not accustomed. The poor chap was set up to fire bullets from a gun that someone else had loaded! Clubs and the County Union generated some of these problems by arranging Scratch League Matches on the same weekend as a County match. These local conflicts were rapidly resolved, by friendly discussion between those players who love golf. Conrad still appears occasionally to support golf, most notably at the Union's seventy five-year celebration event at Wellingborough G.C. where he joined the celebrations. His father Jo would have been proud of his commitment, which mirrored how hard Jo worked for the company J.T.C. Surveys and his drive to assist in developing Conrad's golfing potential.

*Golfing sensations (from left to right): Robert Faulder,
Colin McKenzie and Glen Thompson.*

*Father Trevor Lloyd with sons Jon (left) and Jamie who have all scored holes in one.*

146

Over the years there have been some remarkable scores recorded by the Juniors, whose handicaps are often tumbling down. The most notable occurred at Kettering Road during the Junior Medal. When young Robert Faulder finished with a nett 60, nine under par, he could easily have expected to win. But 14-year-old Robert could only manage third place. Five shots behind Glen Thompson and a staggering twelve shots behind 13 year-old Colin Mackenzie who shot an incredible nett 48. The best scores the Club could remember for a Junior was nett 57, but the rounds they turned in were equivalent to nine, 14 and 21 under par. Colin's handicap was reduced from 36 to 20 after his spectacular round by a stunned Junior Organiser Brian Ollive.

In 1987 on the way back from a Junior match against Staverton Park some of the players decided to bare their bottoms out of the bus window, totally unaware that Brian Ollive the Junior Organiser was driving behind! After the 1989 Northants County Junior Open, Messrs Lloyd, Lloyd and Harris were playing a few more holes. Spotting some balls in the water on the fifteenth, Jon stripped down to his boxer shorts and waded in! When approached by some members, Robert Harris said that they were looking for a club, promptly dropping Jamie's brand new Lynx 3 Iron into the water for Jon to retrieve. Despite Trevor Lloyd driving his sons back to the spot the following morning at 5.30 a.m. the club has not yet materialised to this date. Boys will be boys!

In 1988 Heather Young showed the boys how it should be done by finishing first in the nett competition of the Four Counties Championship at Cold Ashby G.C. and finished second the following year at Cannock Park, Lincs.

At Kettering Road there were several breakages involving Junior members, Simon Tootell managed to hit the Captain's car from the first tee after hitting the ladies tee block. Andrew Harrison was on the receiving end of a full-blooded swing from his playing partner Daniel Tyler thus relieving him of a couple of teeth! A similar incident, without the loss of teeth, involved Gary Tootell and his dad, Ray. Thankfully Gary suffered nothing worse than a bloodied nose. Gary was also responsible for smashing the wing mirror of a passing motorist after volleying the ball over the clubhouse after missing a short putt.

Following the move to Harlestone the Juniors found the course to be a more demanding test due to its increased length and the difficulties of the three lake holes. I particularly remember my son, Alex, saying with tears in his eyes, " It's not bloody fair! I have to play the eighteenth across the bridge, it's costing me shots". As a fragile eight year-old who had just been promoted from the nine hole mini-medals, he could not carry the water in 1992 he can almost drive the green now!

A Junior member recorded the first ever hole in one at Harlestone, when Jamie Lloyd aced the 13th hole on the 13th December1990, age (you guessed it) 13 with a five iron.

The early years at our new Club, up to 1995, witnessed the development of our young lads. Jason Osborne described it as, "the transformation of some spotty kids in to some fine low handicap golfers". Many of these "spotty kids" now make up the bulk of the Club's Scratch and Hollingsworth teams with a few experienced old boys such as Jason et al. Some of these players were very keen on their golf. Club Captain Brian Ollive, himself a past Junior Organiser, had the unpleasant task of telling the Junior's off for ruining the putting green. Their crime? Practising so much, that the putting green was becoming worn out! In a similar vein, Alex Wray played around the lake prior to the Junior medal, promptly scored nett 65 and was disqualified by the Junior Organiser for practising on the course.

On the competitive scene Peterborough Milton has not been a happy hunting ground for the lads. Daniel Beames bought a dozen new balls and promptly lost them all on the front nine. Grant Stewart was playing in the mid-Anglian Junior Open and had such a torrid time that he decided to walk in. When approached by a cross Junior Organiser, Trevor Lloyd, asking for an explanation, Grant's reply was simple: " I can't carry on. I haven't got any balls left" . Gary Tootell (again!) "let go" of his pitching wedge on the sixteenth only to see it disappear in to dense undergrowth. Having completed his round and with the help of six colleagues the offending item was recaptured just before darkness.

*Junior A.G.M. at Kettering Road 1987. Left to Right: Harold Shenfield, President; Brian Ollive, Junior Organiser; Roger Starmer, Captain; Keith Bass, N.G.U. Junior Organiser.*

Kettering Golf Club was a happier hunting ground especially for Ed Barham who displayed true grit scoring 112 + 113 and won a prize for completing the course rather than two NRs, a lesson to all juniors and adults alike. Some say that NR stands for No Respect! Around this time Northampton Golf Club supplied 6 of the 10 players for the County Boys' Team in the form of Nigel Harris, Glenn Keates, Jon Lloyd, Damon Shrive, Simon Tootell and the late Robert Harris. In 1994 the Club's team of Nigel Harris, Glenn Keates and Jon Lloyd won the gross prize at the Mid –Anglian Junior Open by a massive 17 shots when they finished 1st, 2nd and 3rd in the individual competition. The lads also featured well in the Nett competition, which was some going since they all had a handicap of four or less.

In the last five years at Harlestone the Club has attracted many promising young players, although I see no real reason to limit the number of Juniors to seventy-five. Let's get them in and on to the course! Those formative years really build the golfing character. For example, shank of the year in 2000 must be awarded to Simon (SJ) Bunn, who managed to hit his ball over the clubhouse in to the car park when attempting to play "a soft floater"

Kelly Hanwell played some superb golf in 1996 and 1997 when she became: –
- County Girls' Champion for the fourth time.
- Semi-Finalist in the English Girls' Championships and represented England at The Home Internationals
- English Schools Champion 1997 scoring 149 at Sherwood Forest G.C. and represented English Schools against Scotland and Wales.
- Daily Mail finalist at Lake Nona Florida USA 1997
- A County Ladies Player to date

Kelly returned in 2001 from her American golf scholarship where she become the Midland Ladies Champion at the tender age of twenty two, beating L. Day of Worcestershire in the final. During a fine spell of play Kelly set a new ladies course record at Harlestone of 71 gross and reduced her handicap to two. Continuing the ladies theme, Sarah Carter developed from the Junior section in to a fine player and has won the County Ladies Championship three times to date and played a major part in the ladies team.

At County level the Club has been well represented in the various trophies the boys compete for during their summer holidays. We have won the Irish Trophy for the best three gross scores in 1996 & 1998, the Scottish Cup for the best three Nett scores six times between 1986-2001 and the Shoe and Leather Cup for the best two Nett also six times in the same period.

The lads did very well in the Junior League in 1996&7 where they represented the Club beautifully, despite losing twice to Collingtree Park

*T. C. A. Knight, C. R. Ceislewicz and Dick Coogen on the ninth fairway at Kettering Road, c.1972.*

*Junior Northampton Cup Winner 2001 Andrew Beeby.*

*Junior Charity Day 1986 at Kettering Road. Left to Right: Jon Lloyd, Jean MacKenzie and Charles Peacock.*

150

G.C. The finals were played at Overstone and Wellingborough G.C.'s where the team lost narrowly by 3.5/2.5 and in a Captain's play-off. Many players from these teams, such as Gavin Condon, Alex Wray and Alex Izzard, have subsequently gone on to represent the Club at much higher levels, a testament to the passion of the Junior Organisers.

Past Junior Champion and Club Champion in 1997, Jon Lloyd has recently become the Junior Organiser in 2001 and is becoming an effective administrator. Who knows, perhaps he will follow in his father's footsteps and become Club Captain in years to come? We look forward to his speech at the Junior A.G.M. and a fun and successful golfing summer for all the Juniors.

# WORLD, NATIONAL, REGIONAL & COUNTY HONOURS FOR PAST AND PRESENT NORTHAMPTON JUNIORS 1969-2001

**England Boys International**
Conrad Ceislewicz 1972

**England Girls International**
Kelly Hanwell 1996

**English Schools Champion**
Kelly Hanwell 1997

**Midland Ladies Champion**
Kelly Hanwell 2001

**Anglian League A Team**
Conrad Ceislewicz 1972
Martin Izzard 1990

**Anglian League B Team**
Kevin Newman 1980
Martin Izzard 1980

**County Champions Men**
*StrokePlay*
Conrad Ceslewicz
1973,1975,1978,1979,1980
Glenn Keates1998
*Matchplay*
Glenn Keates 2000

**County Champions Ladies**
Sarah Carter 1996, 1997, 2001
Heather Young (Girls) 1990,1991
Kelly Hanwell (Girls) 1993,1995,1996

**County Champions Boys**
Conrad Ceislewicz 1971&2
Tim Giles 1973
Alex Izzard 2000

**County Open Champion**
Tim Giles 1987

**County Higgs Bowl**
Chris Westall 1970
Glenn Cottrell 1999

**County Stableford Cup**
Martin Izzard & Adrian Peacock 1997

*151*

**County Family Foursomes**
Gary & Tony Addington 1990
Alex & Martin Izzard 1998

**County Handicap Challenge Cup**
Tim Giles 1976
Conrad Ceislweicz 1978,1979
Colin Mackenzie 1992

**County
President**
Tony Stevens 1990-92
Martin Izzard 1996-8

**British Transplant
Champion**
Alex Wray 2000

**World Transplant
Champion (Swimming)**
Alex Wray 2001

# Junior Honours

| Year | Junior Organiser | Junior Captain |
|------|------------------|----------------|
| 1971 | B. MILNER | |
| 1972 | G. SIBLEY | |
| 1979-85 | B.MEADOWS | |
| 1986 | B.OLLIVE | I.HEATH |
| 1987 | B.OLLIVE | A.J.PEACOCK |
| 1988 | B.OLLIVE & D.DARE | R.J.FAULDER |
| 1989 | T.LLOYD | R.T.F.WILLOUGHBY |
| 1990 | T.LLOYD | D.A.SHRIVE |
| 1991 | T.LLOYD | M.P.HENDERSON |
| 1992 | T.LLOYD | J.M.LLOYD |
| 1993 | J.COOPER | S.J.BUNN |
| 1994 | S.TROUT & C.OAKENFULL | I.P.JONES |
| 1995 | S.TROUT & C.WOOD | Miss K.M.HANWELL |
| 1996 | S.TROUT & C.WOOD | G.P.CONDON |
| 1997 | S.TROUT & C.WOOD | S.J.VALLANCE |
| 1998 | C.WOOD & S.BLACKAMORE | M.WESTLEY |
| 1999 | M.PEPPER | N.AMBIDGE |
| 2000 | M.PEPPER | G.KNIGHT |
| 2001 | J.M.LLOYD | A.J.IZZARD |
| 2002 | J.M.LLOYD | D.KENNEDY |

# SINGLES TROPHIES

| YEAR | BOYS TROPHY (1)<br>GROSS | BOYS TROPHY (2)<br>NETT | GIRLS TROPHY (3)<br>NETT |
|------|------------------|-----------------|------------------|
| 1964 | P.STILES | | |
| 1965 | C.CEISLEWICZ | | |
| 1966 | C.CEISLEWICZ | | |
| 1967 | N.DURANT | | |
| 1968 | C.WESTALL | | |
| 1969 | T.GILES | | |
| 1970 | R.LOVELADY | | |
| 1971 | T.COOK | | |
| 1972 | C.CEISLEWICZ | | |
| 1973 | W.BINGHAM | | |
| 1974 | P.McGILLIVRAY | | |
| 1975 | D.MINOR | | |
| 1976 | D.GARDNER | | |
| 1977 | L.RUSSELL | | |
| 1978 | J.SMITH | | |
| 1979 | T.PANTHER | | |
| 1980 | M.HOWKINS | | |
| 1981 | M.PANTHER | | |
| 1982 | M.ORAM | | |
| 1983 | G.KIERAN | | |
| 1984 | D.WEBSTER | | |
| 1985 | R.PARKER | | C.HOPE |
| 1986 | C.MacKENZIE | | S.CARTER |
| 1987 | J.M.LLOYD | | NC |
| 1988 | N.MOORCROFT | | NC |
| 1989 | D.ROBERTS | | NC |
| 1990 | G.H.KEATES | | K.HANWELL |
| 1991 | G.H.KEATES | J.W.LLOYD | K.HANWELL |
| 1992 | N.HARRIS | M.HENDERSON | T.COOPER |
| 1993 | S.P.TOOTELL | N.TAYLOR | G.TROUT |
| 1994 | S.P.TOOTELL | G.CONDON | R.TAYLOR |
| 1995 | S.P.TOOTELL | S.P.TOOTELL | K.HANWELL |
| 1996 | G.CONDON | G.CONDON | V.SUTHERLAND |
| 1997 | A.J.IZZARD | A.J.IZZARD | NC |
| 1998 | S.D.PEPPER | S.D.PEPPER | A.McARTHUR |
| 1999 | A.J.IZZARD | G.KNIGHT | G.BUSTIN |
| 2000 | S.D.PEPPER | S.FRESHWATER | A.McARTHUR |
| 2001 | A.J.IZZARD | M.HOWES | M.LINNETT |

1.Presented by Horace Lacey

2. Presented by Mrs A.Wood Lady Captain 1991

3. Presented by the Carter Family.     NC Not Contested

| YEAR | SUMMER KNOCKOUT | JUNIORS TROPHY | WINTER LEAGUE |
|------|-----------------|----------------|---------------|
| 1971 | M.J.IZZARD | | |
| 1972 | A.PAINTIN | | |
| 1973 | K.NEWMAN | | |
| 1974 | A.NASH | | |
| 1975 | L.RUSSELL | | |
| 1976 | NC | | |
| 1977 | NC | | |
| 1978 | NC | | |
| 1979 | A.MEADOWS | | |
| 1980 | R.PRIOR | S.GRAHAM | M.BRITTEN |
| 1981 | D.GORE | P.BOWEN | R.PRIOR |
| 1982 | T.PANTHER | G.P.ADDINGTON | M.JELLEY |
| 1983 | K.RAGBIR | T.R.ADDINGTON | M.GREEN |
| 1984 | A.PEACOCK | M.JELLEY | A.J.PEACOCK |
| 1985 | G.ADDINGTON | P.WARD | C.HOPEWELL |
| 1986 | R.FAULDER | M.SAUNDERSON | C.MacKENZIE |
| 1987 | P.STONES | R.T.F.WILLOUGHBY | S.BAILEY |
| 1988 | M.SAUNDERSON | M.HENDERSON | P.STONES |
| 1989 | D.SHRIVE | D.ROBERTS | D.SHRIVE |
| 1990 | G.TOOTELL | B.HINTON | S.P.TOOTELL |
| 1991 | G.TOOTELL | R.PAGE | S.P.TOOTELL |
| 1992 | R.PAGE | R.HARRIS | A.HARRISON |
| 1993 | G.CONDON | A.WEBSTER | NC |
| 1994 | G.CONDON | G.STEWART | S.P.TOOTELL |
| 1995 | S.P.TOOTELL | S.P.TOOTELL | S.P.TOOTELL |
| 1996 | N.AMBIDGE | A.BASHAM | NC |
| 1997 | A.MILNE | B.NICKELS | A.J.IZZARD |
| 1998 | N.AMBIDGE | G.PARKER | A.MILNE |
| 1999 | NC | D.KENNEDY | A.J.IZZARD |
| 2000 | NC | NC | NC |
| 2001 | NC | A.BEEBY | NC |

| YEAR | ABBOTT BOWL | HARES CUP (1) | RABBITS CUP |
|------|-------------|---------------|-------------|
| 1979 | | R.HOLDING | D.CURTIS |
| 1980 | | M.JELLEY | M.J.GREEN |
| 1981 | | W.RAGBIR | P.BOWEN |
| 1982 | | J.UNDERWOOD | T.R. ADDINGTON |
| 1983 | | P.BOWEN | J.CURREY |
| 1984 | | J.CURREY | D.WEBSTER |
| 1985 | R.PARKER | G.MERRYFIELD | N.J.FROST |
| 1986 | G.P.ADDINGTON | D.HALL | J.WARD |
| 1987 | R.FAULDER | D.SHRIVE | N.LARKIN |
| 1988 | M.HEATH | D.GLASS | M.HENDERSON |

| 1989 | R.T.F.WILLOUGHBY | D.ROBERTS | S.P.TOOTELL |
|------|------------------|-----------|-------------|
| 1990 | J.M.LLOYD | S.P.TOOTELL | G.SMITH |
| 1991 | G.H.KEATES | I.ISGAR | S.J.VALLANCE |
| 1992 | N.HARRIS | D.TYLER | G.CONDON |
| 1993 | K.HANWELL | D.TYLER | G.ROBERTSON |
| 1994 | S.P.TOOTELL | NC | G.PARKER |
| 1995 | K.HANWELL | A.J.IZZARD | S.PEPPER |
| 1996 | G.CONDON | D.KENNEDY | P.BASHAM |
| 1997 | S.VALLANCE | G.PARKER | A.MATTACOLA |
| 1998 | N.AMBIDGE | G.KNIGHT | T.WYKES |
| 1999 | S.PEPPER | C.CROOK | L.ADDINGTON |
| 2000 | G.KNIGHT | B.NICKELS | T.D.LINNETT |
| 2001 | A.J.IZZARD | C.BONE | E.SLINN |

1. Presented by T.J.Lloyd Captain 1994

| YEAR | ECLECTIC SALVERS (1) GROSS | ELECTIC SALVERS NETT | JUNIOR CHARITY DAY (2) | JUNIOR CAPTAIN'S DAY (3) | ROBERT HARRIS CUP (4) |
|------|------|------|------|------|------|
| 1986 | | | S.BAILEY | | |
| 1987 | | | R.FAULDER | | |
| 1988 | | | D.SHRIVE | | |
| 1989 | | | D.HILLIER | M.HENDERSON | |
| 1990 | J.M.LLOYD 59 | J.W.LLOYD 59 | M.HENDERSON | G.H.KEATES | |
| 1991 | J.M.LLOYD 55 | G.H.KEATES 60.5 | | S.P.TOOTELL | A.HARRISON |
| 1992 | J.M.LLOYD 60 | J.W.LlOYD 59.5 | A.P.WRAY | NC | |
| 1993 | J.M.LLOYD 57 | S.J.BUNN 58.5 | G.CONDON | NC | |
| 1994 | S.P.TOOTELL 62 | I.JONES 60 | S.J.VALLANCE | E.BARHAM | G.CONDON |
| 1995 | S.P.TOOTELL 68 | S.J.VALLANCE 60.5 | A.P.WRAY | M.WESTLEY | D.SNAPES |
| 1996 | S.VALLANCE 66 | K.HANWELL 63 | A.J.IZZARD | A.J.IZZARD | A.BASHAM |
| 1997 | S.VALLANCE | N.AMBIDGE | N.AMBIDGE | NC | S.PEPPER |
| 1998 | A.J.IZZARD | G.PARKER | G.KNIGHT | P.TEE & A.MATTACOLA | D.KENNEDY |
| 1999 | A.J.IZZARD | P.TEE | D.KENNEDY | NC | S.D.PEPPER |
| 2000 | S.D.PEPPER | T.M.WYKES | D.KENNEDY | A.J.IZZARD | A.J.IZZARD |
| 2001 | A.J.IZZARD | C.PAGE | C.PAGE | E.SHEPHERD | M.HOWES |

1. Presented by Travis Perkins in 1990.
2. Presented by B.J.Meadows Captain 1986 and Mrs M.Panter Lady Captain 1986.
3. Presented by Brian (Captain 1991) and Paula Ollive 1989.
4. Presented by Martin and Sue Harris 1993.

*Junior A.G.M. 1987 – 'How many members do you recognise?'*

*N.G.U. Junior League Finalists 1996 at Overstone Park, Left to Right: A. J. Izzard,*
*A. P. Wray, N. Ambidge, G. Condon, S. J. Vallance, D. Snapes, M. Westley.*

*156*

# PAIRS TROPHIES

| YEAR | SUMMER FOURSOMES (1) | WINTER FOURSOMES (2) | LADIES & JUNIOR SHIELD |
|---|---|---|---|
| 1985 | | C.HOPEWELL M.ORAM | |
| 1986 | | A.PEACOCK G.P.ADDINGTON | |
| 1987 | | P.STONES M.HEATH | R.FAULDER Mrs J.FELL |
| 1988 | | P.STONES M.HEATH | C.LANE Mrs M.FROST |
| 1989 | | P.STONES M.HEATH | G.TOOTELL Mrs B.JOHNSON |
| 1990 | R.HARRIS S.P.TOOTELL | M.HENDERSON S.P.TOOTELL | G.TOOTELL Mrs M.MIDDLETON |
| 1991 | R.HARRIS S.P.TOOTELL | G.H.KEATES D.SHRIVE | S.P.TOOTELL Mrs M.MIDDLETON |
| 1992 | NC | J.W.LLOYD S.J.BUNN | G.STEWART Mrs C.OAKENFULL |
| 1993 | I.JONES S.P.TOOTELL | NC | R.PAGE Mrs G.COOPER |
| 1994 | G.CONDON A.P.WRAY | I.JONES S.P.TOOTELL | N.AMBIDGE Mrs V.WHITE |
| 1995 | A.J.IZZARD S.J.VALLANCE | NC | A.BASHAM Mrs V.WHITE |
| 1996 | G.CONDON A.P.WRAY | A.J.IZZARD S.J.VALLANCE | L.TELLING Mrs J.PEACOCK |
| 1997 | NC | A.J.IZZARD S.J.VALLANCE | A.BASHAM Mrs J.PEACOCK |
| 1998 | G.KNIGHT S.D.PEPPER | NC | S.D.PEPPER Mrs. A.ARMITAGE |
| 1999 | NC | NC | T.WYKES Mrs J.WOODS |
| 2000 | NC | NC | NC |
| 2001 | A.BEEBY M.HOWES | | S.WILSON Mrs.V.WHITE |

1. Presented by David (Captain 1990) and Jean Prior 1990.
2. Presented by John Eyton-Jones President 1991.

*Junior Supporters for the 1996 League Final: Sylvia Trout, Julie Starmer, Kelly Hanwell, Richard & Jeannie Craddock and Judy Keates at Overstone.*

*County Inter Club Team Championship Winners 1999, Left to Right: A. J. Izzard, T. Wykes, N. Ambidge, G. Knight, D. Kennedy, S. D. Pepper, S. Freshwater, P. Tee, seated at Collingtree Park.*

# CHAPTER 33

# The Millenium Trophy

"Golf is based on honesty, where else would you admit to a seven on a par three"

Jimmy Demaret

THIS trophy was presented to the Club by the Northampton Golf Club Company Ltd to celebrate the Millenium and also to mark the passing away (10/02/2000) of a great Club stalwart Harold Shenfield, who supported the Club to an age of eighty eight. Harold was a great lover of foursomes golf, fittingly this trophy is played as a foursomes stableford off three eighths of the player's combined handicap. Three eighths being traditionally favored against the English Golf Union's recently recommended half of combined total. As previously described in Chapter 15, this is a wonderful format for golf especially on a cold winters day when the course can be completed in a relatively short time. Back at Kettering road, foursomes was a much commoner form of golf as the record books from the sixties and seventies show, greensomes being particularly favoured.

This marvellous trophy is played for in the summer months often on a bank holiday, where it is open to all categories of membership. On it's first outing the trophy was won by Frank Bustin and D.Adams with a score of 35 points. In 2001 the trophy was won by father and son, Carl and Simon Williams, with a score of 35 points, beating Andy Carter and Jon Lloyd by a single point.

*Millennium Trophy Winners: D. Adams and F. Bustin with Club Captain A. R. G. Harrison.*

# CHAPTER 34

# The Kettering Road Course...Lets remember it!

" Don't play too much golf......two rounds a day is plenty"

Harry Vardon.

**HERE is a well established course which by its very nature will attract visitors to play it time and again, for the Northampton course has to be learned and its hills and hollows have to be harnessed to the player's skill. Founded in 1893 the original nine holes were situated over two fields in Weston Favell, but this was dull stuff and the founder members soon found land which was ideal from a golf architect's point of view and perfect as a centrifugal point, where buses from the town and outlying districts converge and set the players down almost in the club house.**

The terrain known locally as "the Hills and Hollows" or "Little Switzerland" got its amazingly undulating contours from ancient quarrying for ironstone. These velvety excrescencies which are almost volcanic in effect gave every type of lie imaginable and provide the players with the utmost variety of shots. Uphill or hanging lies were the order of the day for the first few holes with entrancing greens tucked away amongst the miniature pyramids.

Later the course took on a more urban and orthodox appearance but every hole demanded thought and skill if par figures were to be produced.

There are many doglegs and the FIRST (430 yards) sets the pattern. We drive as near an out of bounds hedge to the left as we dare so as to open the closely guarded green for a long second shot. The green was slightly plateau and we felt a deserved glow of pride when we make it in two shots.

The SECOND hole (305 yards) had a green set in the hillocks with three cross-bunkers just short of it. A very long drive might be trapped in one of these, but an average length skilfully placed gave the opportunity of a delight-ful approach to a hole was anything but obvious.

The short THIRD, a mere 161 yards, was played from a plateau tee and was simplicity itself with the wind behind us, but a cross wind made it difficult to find the green tucked away in a hollow

The long FOURTH (439 yards) had another of those attractive plateau tees. The farm with its trees (in 1965) lies waiting for a hook or gorse bushes invite a slice. There is nothing for it but to open our shoulders to a good straight drive and try to reach level ground. Then we may reach the green guarded on all sides with sand and grass bunkers if we hit our second shot firmly.

The FIFTH "Braid's" was an uphill hole of 480 yards calling for power more than anything else. A wide fairway allowed plenty of latitude but a good pitch was necessary to land on the slightly raised green. Avoid the small pond from the stream's outflow on the left close to the green near the willow tree. After this effort we have the respite of the downhill SIXTH (497 yards) a

*The daunting approach to the first green.*

*The second tee with a good carry over the 'hills and hollows'.*

straight forward hole with a lateral water hazard on the right, out of bounds in the farm yard and many bunkers which could trap a poor second shot.

The SEVENTH was a gem of a short hole. Only 134 yards and from a raised tee, but we must be on the postage stamp green or nowhere for it is surrounded by no fewer than seven pot bunkers.

The EIGHTH (391 yards) was uphill and it is well to drive to the left and so get in the best position for the shot to the green over the cross bunkers which are about 30 yards short. There were also deep bunkers on each side of the green.

The NINTH was a most intriguing downhill hole of 421 yards. The drive was through a narrow gap between trees and though the fairway was generous, there was a crop of gorse bushes in the direct line to the green. With a following wind these were easy to carry but with the wind against, it was well to play short and rely on an accurate pitch. (Sadly the trees which created the tiny gap were lost to Dutch Elm disease in nineteen seventies which completely changed the character of the hole).

*John Costin tees off on the fourth at Kettering Road.*

*The fourth green with the fairway and sixteenth hole in the background.*

*View from behind the eighth green with the sixth and eighth fairways left and right.*

The TENTH was a fascinating short hole. Only 164 yards, there was a hollow in front of the green rather like the "Valley of Sin" at St.Andrews. A good 4 iron was necessary to land on the closely guarded green. Do not go through the green or a hard chip will be left.

The ELEVENTH (322 yards) had another delightful plateau tee. We played to the left to open the way to a small green guarded by a steep bunker.

The dogleg (385 yards) TWELFTH had cross-bunkers that could trap a good drive. The handicap man wisely played short and there was a clump of trees on the left, which had to be avoided. The green had one very deep sloped bunker on the left-hand side, which must be avoided.

The (331 yards) THIRTEENTH was an easy straightforward hole. We held the ball slightly to the right and keep clear of all trouble.

The (167 yards) FOURTEENTH was another excellent short hole, where with the prevailing wind no difficulties should arise providing we hole the ball to the right and so keep out of the bunkers left of the sloping green.

*The thirteenth hole.*

*The pitch to the sixteenth green.*

We are now getting back to the hills and hollows. The FIFTEENTH (390 yards) had the last of the downhill drives and apart from an out of bounds on the left there are no special difficulties apart from the big poplar trees which would block out the second shot from a pushed drive.

The (333 yards) SIXTEENTH "Broomfield's" was a very different story. Here was a hole worthy of any championship course where the expert can open his shoulders and play a fine drive to the left in readiness for a pitch to a plateau green with a yawning bunker below it. Anyone unfortunate enough to land in this steeply banked bunker could all too easily get into another guarding the green and double figures were often collected here.

The (197 yards) SEVENTEENTH was a long shotter among the hills and hollows, which was further, complicated by bushes. The saucer shaped green was steeply banked at the front and protected to the right by a large two-tier mound. A good shot slightly to the left was usually carried in the right direction down the slopes towards the hole. In years gone by, this green or a green similar one to it, was played as the second hole in Tom Morris and Norman Dawson's 1894 layout but from a tee close to the Kettering Road as a 220 yards bogey four.

The (455 yards) EIGHTEENTH was doglegged and furnished with a kindly plateau tee. A long drive left of the hillocks and hollows opened the big green which looks like an emerald island surrounded by seven bunkers. The green had out of bounds to the left and beyond, which contributed to what was arguably one of the most difficult second shots to any final hole in the County.

*The sixteenth green.*

*The demanding tee shot to the 197-yard seventeenth hole over Little Switzerland.*

*Tee shot at the most difficult finishing hole in Northamptonshire – the 455-yard dogleg eighteenth.*

And so to the hospitality and comfortable clubhouse after a round over most unusual and interesting terrain. Tea and toast for two please Mrs Wilkinson, when you are free!

*Adapted by the author from The 1969 N.G.C. Official Handbook by Betty Debenham. Annual subscription £18, weekday green fees with a member ten shillings or £2 for a whole week!*

Having played at Kettering Road from 1969 to 1990 my eclectic score gradually came down to 41 (18 under par) scoring 3,2,2,3,3,3,2,3,2 =23 + 1,2,3,2,2,2,2,1,3 =18. During my research for this book, former club member and county stalwart Richard Aitken holds the lowest eclectic score I have discovered of 40 (21 under par). He amassed this record between 1969-2001 at Church Brampton scoring a remarkable 3,3,1,2,2,1,2,2,3 = 19 + 3,3,1,3,2,2,3,2,2 = 21. Is there a better set of scores out there on any Northamptonshire course? Please let me know.

*Dave Eborall puts out on the last day the Kettering Road course was open, the 5 Oct 1990 watched by Alan Parker and Jack Turner.*

*Summer view of the eighteenth fairway at Kettering Road c.1980*

# CHAPTER 35

# Club Professionals

"The reason the pro tells you to keep your head down is so you can't see him laughing ".

Phyllis Diller

**THE old Club had a very welcoming and encouraging professional for young Junior golfers in Alf Lovelady. Alf has a wide knowledge of the game and one of the silkiest swings around and was always a reference point for golf information and encouragement. As a fourteen-year-old in 1969 I was surprised and somewhat embarrassed to be "fitted out" with a set of ladies woods which were described as being just right for me. Alf's recommendation was, of course correct, as my young swing was not yet ready for a set of stiff-shafted woods. The eleventh at Kettering road needed a drive and a four wood for me to reach it in my young days. His thirty-two years as professional between 1954 to 1986 allowed him to become a well-respected and popular figure around the Club.**

There was a cheeky, cheerful assistant in the old shop at the top of the car park who had a real desire for the game and turned in to a fine player. Mike Gallagher had a superb short game and played in The Open Championship. During my summer holidays Mike was always ready for an evening game after his duties in the shop. Despite the fact that we had played golf all day Mike would "bribe" us with the offer of fish and chips if we would go out for another nine holes. As poor schoolboys we did not often refuse! One of Mike's favorite stories involved the burly six foot four Kingsthorpe character Trev McAlistair and Eddie Addington. Whilst they were walking from the fourteenth green to the fifteenth tee at the old course, a bet on driving the green on this 390 yard hole was struck. Could big Trev drive it with a soft Price's Everlasting golf ball to win Eddie's golf clubs? Trev smashed the ball with great power, which was seen to go over the small ridge just short of the green much to Eddie's horror. Assuming he had driven the green and won the bet, Trev triumphantly carried Eddie's clubs on his shoulder all the way down the fairway to the green, only to discover the ball one foot short of the putting surface. Much to Eddie's relief, Trev threw Eddie's clubs to the ground in disgust and left the course in the direction of The Pioneer, the nearest public house!

Alf Lovelady's son Richard took over in 1986 during a phase when the Club was preparing plans to move from Kettering Road to Harlestone. Richard was and still is a fine ball striker and currently lives in Southern Spain where he has easily adjusted to the pace of Andalucian life. Richard was the only player I have seen drive the ball in to the top bunker from the normal tee on Kettering road's 333 yard 16th hole.

Mark Chamberlain took over from Richard in 1989 and became part of the move to our superb location at Harlestone. Mark was a player with great hands, who could work the ball right to left or left to right as required. This is typified in his description of Harlestone's seventeenth hole, which "requires a draw in to the pin with an eight iron". Mark had a great interest in the history of the game and had a good memory for golfing facts and figures. Mark's two sons now play at Cold Ashby and are very competitive with a lot of embedded experience on their young heads.

The current incumbent Kevin Dickens had a fine record as a tournament professional and is arguably the best playing professional at the Club during my lifetime. He in fact finished second in the 1989 Belgian Open at Royal Waterloo. Kevin has made an enormous impact upon the local golf scene where he fre-quently has been observed collecting significant prizes such as the N.G.U Open, on three occasions, together with many local and Midland events. At the Club, Kevin has taken Peter Huntley all the way to winning the Volvo Club Captain Pro challenge at Wentworth in 1996, which included a chip in for a winning eagle on the eighteenth hole. Kevin was also a member of the 1998 GB&I PGA Cup Team at Colorado Springs who put up a valiant performance against a strong USA team. His sense of humour can be widely appreciated in his excellent verbal impersonation of Seve when he is in the mood!

*Kevin Dickens, Northamptonshire Open Champion 1997 with John Pulford.*

# CHAPTER 36

# Short Strokes, Characters, Stories and Memories

"Eighteen holes of match-play will teach you more about your foe than nineteen years of dealing with him across the desk"

Grantland Rice

## Albatrosses

MY first recollection of this elusive bird was the two albatross twos recorded by the flamboyant Dick Walton at the old course on the par five sixth hole. He was the sort of player who came from the Jerry Fell mould, in that he could play every shot in the book but never knew when it was likely to happen! Players from this mould can make an albatross or miss the ball completely. I am sure his cellmates enjoyed his recollection of these events as he spent some time courtesy of Her Majesty's pleasure.

Young Jamie (Gunner) Lloyd at the tender age of fifteen recorded the new courses first albatross outrageously on the six hundred yard twelfth hole, a feat that will probably never be equalled.

Scott Bailey during winter conditions also managed this feat on the third hole at the new course in heavy fog on a temporary green. The fourball originally thought that the ball was lost in the trees until the hole was inspected just in case!

## Club Stewards and Staff

John (garden gnome) Coles made a friendly welcome to the Club where he became largely instrumental in training R.T.F. Willoughby in the art of bar management. He was steward during the last years at the old Club and produced many delightful dishes from the poorly-equipped and cramped kitchen. His photo gallery of his staff's pieces of anatomy was a delight to the eye, especially the one of Mimi in her suspenders. Mimi became a character from behind the bar where she had the male members guessing as to whether or not she was "clad in bloomers."

Chris Watson, who held the job for a short period at Kettering road, was quite a character. I remember him turning up for work in a very smart suit with soaking wet hair. As he made his way up and down the bar it soon became apparent that he was in fact soaked to the skin having been thrown in to the swimming pool at Skew Bridge Ski Club. He was gradually drying out, as he performed his duties until a resourceful the late Mike Shelford decided to rehydrate him with the total contents of a soda siphon. Unbeknown to many customers prior to being thrown in to the pool, Chris had the weekly bar takings tucked away in his back pocket. All the notes were subsequently hung up all around the kitchen like the weekly washing to be dried.

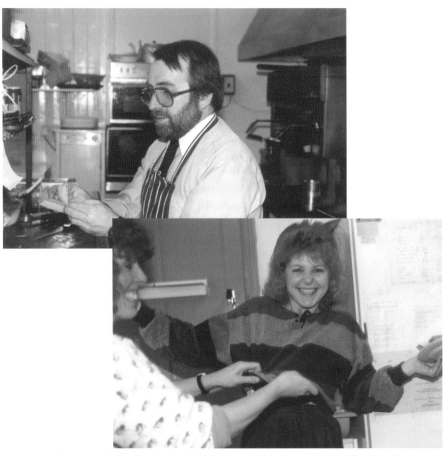

*John Coles at work in the kitchen ably assisted by his wife Pauline and Mimi.*

## Golfing Groups

At the Club there are several groups of like-minded souls, which often holiday together. These include the Hurricanes, the Newarks, the Scratch Mob, the FFrobbers *et al.*

## Scratch Mob

The early trips of the Scratch Mob in 1991 & 2 were notable especially for Andy Carter who through injury had to visit Casualty Department at Glasgow Hospital with a bad back and Kings Lynn Casualty with torn shoulder muscles caused by laughing too much! These golfers play for the famous Blue jacket and trophy, which we could all fit in, to comfortably ten years ago. Nowadays there is no player who can wear the jacket with dignity. This is especially true for the 2001 winner Jon Lloyd. Some stories are best left untold when lads are away, however the following may illustrate how the "team spirit" develops away from home. On leaving a warm pub at closing time to total darkness on a bright moonlit night in North Norfolk one of our party was heard to remark, " Cor that's amazing, there are more stars in Norfolk". As the group walked home down a pitch black village street Glenn Keates and Andy Carter managed to end up wrestling in a pile of pig manure which temporarily resulted in a lost watch and a badly stained jacket. Jeremy Shepherd fell in love with the " Bird in the chip shop" in Scotland before badly cutting his arm when trying to put Glenn Keates head down the toilet, after being locked out of his room in only a towel for one hour. Ex Club professional Richard Lovelady joined us for the trip to Scotland and finished last at golf but first in the bar!

## Famous Shots

(Courtesy of Ron Newman's memory) During an exhibition match at Kettering Road which featured Dave Thomas, Peter Allis, Dai Rees and Alf Lovelady, Dave Thomas's driving was staggering to those watching. His tee shot on the first hole finished on the third green and his tee shot to the 305 yard second hole finished thirty yards through the green and in the hedge, which bordered the course. Both shots measuring around 340 yards. Dai Rees demonstrated his power from the bunker on the eighteenth green near to the clubhouse. The ball was thrown in to the bunker and a member was allowed to stamp on the ball. Dai Rees then took out a five wood and hit the ball amazingly in the allotments to the left of the first fairway, a blow of two hundred yards from a buried lie!

During a Scratch League match in 1995 Peter Owen (Wellingborough G.C.) drove the ball on to the upslope of the 611 yard twelfth hole at Harlestone and reached the green with an eight iron with a strong wind and running conditions. This feat was actually surpassed, by the very powerful player Lee Corfield, from Burnham & Berrow G.C., who put the ball on to the green with a drive and a wedge. This occurred during a practice round for the Midland Open Amateur Championship on the 28/06/2001 with the new Titleist ProVI ball and a Callaway ERC II Trampoline-faced driver. He jokingly admitted that he actually scored five by trying to make an eagle. He is still "putting for dough" and making an impact on the regional golf scene.

During an Anglian League County Match in 1994 Darren Jones (Kingsthorpe G.C.) drove the ball to within a foot of the green on the 456 yard fifteenth hole at the Harlestone course. He unfortunately still lost the match by one hole.

### Holes in One

Hole in one achievements are remarkable, some are extraordinary. One of the most amazing was that of two handicapper Bob Taylor, a member of Scraptoft Golf Club, Leicester and a Leicestershire & Rutland County player. During the practice day for the 1974 Eastern Counties Foursomes on the Hunstanton Links, he holed his tee shot with a 1-iron at the 188-yard 16th. The next day in the first round of the competition, he repeated the feat this time with a six iron since the wind had changed on the tide. When he stepped on to the 16th tee the following day his partner jokingly offered him odds of 1,000,000 to one against holing-in-one for a third successive time. There was a small group of spectator surrounding the green who had gathered just in case. Bob Taylor again selected his six iron and amazingly holed-in-one to the astonishment and cheers of everyone present. I have over the years spoken to several people who were there at the time, they all say it was a though time stopped for a few seconds as they contemplated the significance and improbability of what had just happened. The hole itself is a very difficult par three with a two-tier green and four bunkers and is badly affected by those North Norfolk winds. Bob Taylor became Leicestershire & Rutland County President during the same period that I held that position for Northamptonshire in 1996-98, we have often dined together at functions and chatted about this feat and this beautiful golf course. Poor Bob has become so famous with the story that he is often asked to relive it, since people still find it unbelievable. The bet was in fact taken on jokingly since Bob said " Oh go on then, let's have a penny on it" He is still waiting to be paid by his partner on that famous day in May 1974 and interestingly has not had a hole in one since! An engraved seat has been placed beside the tee by the Club in honour of this magnificent achievement. The odds of achieving a hole in one have been calculated in America to be 3,708 to 1 for a top amateur. Bob Taylor's achievement therefore had a probability of about 50 Billion to 1.

Two holes in one on the same hole on the same day in competitive play in a major tournament-unlikely but true. Over the last two hundred years this had happened less than a handful of times. The latest occurred in

Northamptonshire when North Worcestershire professional Finlay Clark carried out this unique feat last year (2000) at the 14th hole in the Midland PGA Cold Ashby Classic.

The late Stuart Brown is reputed to have also carried out this unique achievement possibly in South Africa.

**Second Hole**
Wally Balshaw 7 Wood, Geoff Bott 5 Iron, Alan Broadbent 4 Iron, Andy Carter 6 Iron, David Dare 5 Wood, Geoff Garbutt 6 Iron, Martin Harris 4 Iron SD, A.Harrison, Derek Hoblin 7 Wood, Ian Jones 8 Iron, Glenn Keates 6 Iron, Charles Peacock 5 Wood.

**Fifth Hole**
Terry Addington 9 Iron, John Basham 9 Iron, G.Blair, Alan Broadbent 8 Iron, Jim Camp-Jones Wedge, Albert Carter 8 Iron, Austin Field 5 Iron, John Gordon 8 Iron, Alan Graham 6 Iron, I.J.Griffiths 6 Iron, John Haddon, Martin Harris Wedge–Twice, Mark Heath Wedge, Paul Hirst Wedge, Martin Izzard 9 Iron, Frank Johnson 8 Iron, A.Lawton 9 Iron, Trevor Lloyd 6 Iron, Maureen Middleton 5 Wood, Peter Miller 8 Iron, Kevin Newman 9 Iron, Andy Nichels 6 Iron, Alan Pardoe 7 Iron, Fred Perkins 8 Iron, John Sadler 9 Iron, Ray Smith 7 Iron, G.Taylor 8 Iron, Joan Peacock 7 Wood.

**Thirteenth Hole**
Bill Bruce 6 Iron, C.Clements 5 Iron, John Danks, Joan Dunn 7 Wood, Ken Elmer 5 Wood, Kelly Hanwell 5 Iron, Frank Hill 7 Iron, Judy Keates 4 Wood, Jamie Lloyd 5 Iron, Jon Lloyd 9 Iron, S.McAurthur, Ben Middleton 9 Iron, Peter Miller 6 Iron, Fred Perkins 5 Wood, S.Pragnell 7 Iron, D.Sayers 6 Iron, Diane Thomas 5 Wood, Ray Tootell 5 Iron, J. McKenzie 5 Wood.

**Sixteenth Hole**
Eddie Addington 6 Iron, Gary Addington 8 Iron, Simon Bunn 5 Iron, Frank Bustin 6 Iron, Gavin Condon 9 Iron, C.Clements 5 Iron, Steve Eborall Wedge, D.Fell 5 Wood, Peter Heath Wedge, Martin Izzard 9 Iron, Neville Kny 5 Wood, S.Parker 9 Iron, Adrian Rudge 9 Iron, Julian Steele 6 Iron, Vera White 7 Iron, Rob Willoughby Wedge SD, Sam pepper 9 Iron.

**Eighteenth Hole**
Vera White 5 Iron.

SD Straight in to the hole

Interestingly of all the holes-in-one recorded at Harlestone Club members Jon Lloyd and Glenn Keates have, along with the author, each observed five of the shots, which have finished in the bottom of the cup.

Can anyone beat this total, or does this reflect the amount of time these players spend playing golf at the Club? Don't tell the wife or girlfriends!

There were two "technical" hole in ones recorded by Peter McKenzie and Jeannie Craddock at the sixteenth hole. They did not need to buy the traditional round of drinks since their first strokes at this hole both finished in the lake!

The most bizarre round of drinks bought for a "technical" hole in one occurred during the County Championship at Church Brampton during the 1970's. Peterborough Milton player Clark McCrae's ball from the old fifteenth tee (now the 6th) was observed to disappear in to the hole by the County Officials watching. Assuming this to be a hole in one, a bar tab was immediately set up in his name. The shot was in fact his provisional ball; the first tee shot being shanked with a three iron on to the adjacent fairway. Before Clark had a chance to pick the ball out of the hole and render it the ball in play (Decision 27-2b/2) his first tee shot was "thoughtfully" found by the group ahead. A pitch to the green and three putts by the shaken player completed the hole.

On returning to the Clubhouse Clark was staggered to find how many new friends he suddenly had, despite his protestations about the score, he sportingly bought the round of drinks having actually scored a double bogey five!

## Course Records

The highly talented Conrad Ceislewicz set the course record at the old Club at three under par 66 in the Boys Championship on the 14th April in 1972 playing with Paul Bingham. Which beat Richard Aitken's and Jim Pettigrew's 1962&1968 scores of 67. I watched Conrad play that day, where he appeared to have total control of power and distance. It was not until the early nineteen eighties that I realised the full significance of what I had witnessed as a seventeen year old.

Andy (NR) Carter in fact equalled the record; this fact has somehow slipped through the record list until now. Andy played with Paul Hirst one summer evening during the July round of the Northampton Cup; he scored 34+32 to equal Conrad's score. His card is reproduced here in this book for it's first public viewing. Two players, James Hallwood and Lance Sloan have stood on the seventeenth tee at four under par only to be denied by bogeys on the very demanding 197 yard seventeenth and the 455 yard eighteenth holes. Mike Gallagher set the professional course record at Kettering Road in 1983 with a fine score of 64 strokes. The score card shows the details of this fine round of golf, Mike's local knowledge gained through many years at the "hills and hollows" must have helped!

Glenn Keates on the 30/08/2001 playing in the 5th round of the Northampton Cup set the amateur course record at Harlestone. His faultless round of 66 included the three birdies on the front nine at the third, sixth and ninth holes and an eagle at the eleventh and a birdie at the seventeenth on

**NORTHAMPTON GOLF CLUB** — Standard Scratch Score 69

| Player A | M. GALLAGHER | Handicap | Strokes | Competition | NORTHANTS P.G.A. STROKE PLAY CHAMPS. |
|---|---|---|---|---|---|
| B | | | | Date | 27/9/83 |

| Markers Score | No. | Yards | Par | Stroke Index | Score A B | Won+ Lost— Halved O Points | Markers Score | No. | Yards | Par | Stroke Index | Score A B | Won+ Lost— Halved O Points |
|---|---|---|---|---|---|---|---|---|---|---|---|---|---|
| | 1 | 430 | 4 | 3 | 4 | | | 10 | 164 | 3 | 15 | 3 | |
| | 2 | 305 | 4 | 14 | 4 | | | 11 | 322 | 4 | 12 | 3 | |
| | 3 | 161 | 3 | 17 | 3 | | | 12 | 385 | 4 | 2 | 4 | |
| | 4 | 439 | 4 | 4 | 4 | | | 13 | 331 | 4 | 13 | 4 | |
| | 5 | 480 | 5 | 11 | 4 | | | 14 | 167 | 3 | 16 | 3 | |
| | 6 | 497 | 5 | 9 | 3 | | | 15 | 390 | 4 | 8 | 4 | |
| | 7 | 134 | 3 | 18 | 3 | | | 16 | 333 | 4 | 7 | 3 | |
| | 8 | 391 | 4 | 1 | 4 | | | 17 | 197 | 3 | 10 | 3 | |
| | 9 | 421 | 4 | 6 | 4 | | | 18 | 455 | 4 | 5 | 4 | |
| | | 3258 | 36 | Out | 33 | | | | 2744 | 33 | In | 31 | |
| | | | | | | | | | 3258 | 36 | Out | 33 | |
| | | | | | | | | | 6002 | 69 | Total | 64 | |

Signature of Marker

Signature of Player

Handicap

Nett Score

---

| Competition | | Date | |
|---|---|---|---|
| Player A | Andy J. Carter | Handicap | 5 |
| Player B | | Handicap | |
| | | Strokes Received | |

| Marker's Score | No. | Yards | Par | Stroke Index | Player's Gross Score A B | Won + Lost – Half 0 Points | Marker's Score | No. | Yards | Par | Stroke Index | Player's Gross Score A B | Won + Lost – Half 0 Points |
|---|---|---|---|---|---|---|---|---|---|---|---|---|---|
| | 1 | 430 | 4 | 3 | 4 | | | 10 | 164 | 3 | 15 | 3 | |
| | 2 | 305 | 4 | 14 | 3 | | | 11 | 322 | 4 | 12 | 3 | |
| | 3 | 161 | 3 | 17 | 4 | | | 12 | 385 | 4 | 2 | 4 | |
| | 4 | 439 | 4 | 4 | 4 | | | 13 | 331 | 4 | 13 | 4 | |
| | 5 | 480 | 5 | 11 | 4 | | | 14 | 167 | 3 | 16 | 3 | |
| | 6 | 497 | 5 | 9 | 4 | | | 15 | 390 | 4 | 8 | 4 | |
| | 7 | 134 | 3 | 18 | 3 | | | 16 | 333 | 4 | 7 | 4 | |
| | 8 | 391 | 4 | 1 | 4 | | | 17 | 197 | 3 | 10 | 3 | |
| | 9 | 421 | 4 | 6 | 4 | | | 18 | 455 | 4 | 5 | 4 | |
| | | 3258 | 36 | Out | 34 | | | | 2744 | 33 | In | 32 | |
| | | | | | | | | | 3258 | 36 | Out | 34 | |
| | | | | | | | | | 6002 | 69 | Total | 66 | |

Standard Scratch Score 69

Marker's Signature

Player's Signature

Handicap — 5

Nett Score — 61

*Mike Gallagher and Andy Carter's Course Records from Kettering Road.*

the back nine. Andy Hare set the professional record also 66, on September 20th 2001 during the Northamptonshire County Union's Autohaus Audi Open. Andy's card contained birdies at the third, fourth and sixth holes on the front nine and birdies on the tenth, sixteenth and eighteenth on the back nine. On this day Andy Carter from the host Club became the 2001 Autohaus Audi Amateur Champion with scores of 75,71 gross where he won the title on countback from four other players on 146, two over par.

The course records at Harlestone currently (Sept 2001) stand at:
Professional 66 A.Hare
Amateur 66 G.H.Keates
Ladies 71 K.Hanwell

## Record Scores, 59 Gross

Northampton golfer Stuart Reynolds from Church Brampton became the first British golfer to ever break the 60 barrier as he fired a stunning 12 under par 59 on the par 71 course to win the Midland PGA pro-am at Burton-on-Trent on the 3rd August 2001. Stuart joins a distinguished handful of golfers including Sam Snead (59 in the1959 Greenbrier Open), Jack Nicklaus (59 in an exhibition match in 1973 at Palm Beach), Al Geiberger (59 in the Danny Thomas Memphis Classic, Colonial Country Club 1977), Chip Beck(59 in the Las Vegas Invitational, 1991), David Duval (59 in the 1999 Bob Hope Chrysler Classic), Shigeki Maruyama(58 in qualifying for US Open 2000 at Woodmont Country Club) Annika Sorenstam (59 Standard Register Ping in Phoenix 2001) and Jason Bohn(58 in the Bayer Championship Huron Oaks Ontario, 2001) who have accomplished this feat in competitive play. His round consisted of two nines of six under par where Stuart started his round from the tenth tee.

| Hole | 1 | 2 | 3 | 4 | 5 | 6 | 7 | 8 | 9 |
|------|-----|-----|-----|-----|-----|-----|-----|-----|-----|
| Par | 4 | 3 | 5 | 5 | 4 | 3 | 4 | 4 | 4 |
| | 359 yds | 140 yds | 548 yds | 489 yds | 454 yds | 165 yds | 384 yds | 366 yds | 379 yds |
| Score | 4 | 2* | 5 | 3** | 3* | 2* | 3* | 4 | 4 |

| Hole | 10 | 11 | 12 | 13 | 14 | 15 | 16 | 17 | 18 |
|------|-----|-----|-----|-----|-----|-----|-----|-----|-----|
| Par | 3 | 4 | 3 | 5 | 4 | 4 | 4 | 4 | 4 |
| | 198 yds | 318 yds | 214 yds | 514 yds | 445 yds | 349 yds | 432 yds | 446 yds | 379 yds |
| Score | 2* | 3* | 3 | 4* | 3* | 3* | 3* | 4 | 4 |

*Birdie ** Eagle

Stuart's putter was extremely hot, especially on the back nine, since he only required 25 putts. The longest one he holed was of twenty feet. In his own words, " I did not really feel nervous at all until the last green when I realised that I had two putts from ten foot for a 59". In golfing terms he literally knocked the stick out and reaped the rewards!

Interestingly of all the players who have scored below sixty, none of them have broken seventy the next time they played.

## Trophies Night Happenings

This celebratory affair is one of the Club's main events during the year and is attended by a large number of winners and supporters. The tradition of filling the trophy to celebrate one's victory ensures that a good variety of beverages are consumed. Only those with the strongest constitution or those with the right will-power survive.

- "Del Boy" Holland drove home, went to bed and left his wife at the Club!
- Grev Faulkner drove up from the bottom car park at the old course and almost flattened a little old lady walking her dog at the entrance to the Club
- Peter Rees fell out of the clubhouse and bent several trophies on the gravel

*The first Trophy Night at Harlestone, November 1990.*

*Simon Bunn shows off his scars from Trophies Night.*

*Centenary, Trophies Night 1993.*

*Bob Frost with a large round of drinks at Trophies Night.*

- Andy "NR" Carter went home "early" at 11 o'clock because his dress watch had not been adjusted for the winter
- Chris Hopewell slept under the snooker table to get rid of the effect of the booze
- Keith Heard decided to drown Andy Carter and Jeremy Shepherd with a pint of beer having been wound up. He did not make the celebrations the following year, which was a shame since the boys had their waterproof jacket and trousers with them for the after meal celebrations.
- Alex Izzard produced a "street pizza" on my mother's carpet because he was "not used to rich food"
- Simon "SJ" Bunn fell into the gravel with "Toots" on his back whilst walking home and dug a bloody hole in his face
- The 1993 Centenary trophies night celebrations went on long into the early hours when one appreciated being part of this unique day where the feelings of those who have gone before us and who have looked after and nurtured this wonderful Club were remembered
- Millennium trophies night was a special night to remember despite the relatively poor turn out of members. There was a good spectrum of ages represented from Junior players through to Seniors, Club officials and the County President, who was very impressed by the fellowship displayed by the members present.

*Keith and Helen Brownless, Joan Peacock and John Basham. Millennium Winners of the Robert Harris Fun-day with Captain A. R. G. (Tony) Harrison, Martin and Sue Harris.*

## Northampton Open 1975

The Club hosted its fifth open competition for golfers with handicaps lower than six from the Midlands area, which was held on 7th June, 1975.The Open was later disbanded, since the players did not conduct themselves in an appropriate manner and were described as money grabbing youths! The field included many now famous golfers, together with local players from the County. The trophy was won by now professional Martin Curry with a total of 141 (69-72). Peter McEvoy now a famous amateur golfer finishing tied for third place on 146, off scratch with the 1985 Northamptonshire County Champion Mike McNally. Andrew Carman now an England selector from Daventry, put in the best performance from the County. The Club's best performance came from John Costin and Chris Westall, who finished tied for twelfth. Interestingly, even with a high-class field including the best ever-amateur golfer in England, no one broke the par of sixty nine and par was only equalled twice. The old "hills and hollows" predictably kept her dignity that day, she was rarely beaten in ninety years of play. Sadly the open was never repeated at the old course. One can merely hypothesise how the new equipment and balls might have challenged the Kettering Road test. I personally do not see a change in the overall scenario in view of the degree of difficulty at the "hills and hollows".

## Daily Mail Amateur Foursomes National Finalists Northamptonshire

This popular competition has been running now for over forty years where players initially qualify as their Club's foursomes champions. There are approximately six local/regional rounds before the competitors battle it out on the national stage over three days of golf and entertainment. For the record the following pairs have qualified from the County where Northampton has been well represented by current and some players who have move to Northants County.

| Year | Gender | Club & Players | Results |
|------|--------|----------------|---------|
| 1965 | Men | Northampton<br>W.Clarke 5, N.B.Jones 5 | Lost to Hazel Grove |
| 1966 | Men | Northampton<br>A.F.Stevens 8, L.A.Johnson 6 | Lost to Royal Epping Forest |
| 1971 | Men | Northants County<br>J.D.Haig 10, R.A.Haig 6 | Lost to Royal Worlington and Newmarket |
| 1974 | Men | Northants County<br>R.G.Halliday 3, A.Bishop 4 | Beat Purley Downs<br>Lost to Gerrards Cross |

| 1979 | Men | Priors Hall<br>N.Dean 6,<br>P.Robinson 14 | Beat Ringway<br>Lost to Scarborough South<br>Cliff |
|------|-----|--------------------|---------------------|
| 1981 | Women | Kingsthorpe<br>Mrs.S.Tookey 12,<br>Mrs P.Coles 13 | Lost to North Wales |
| 1984 | Women | Kettering<br>L.White 7, T.Rolfe 15 | Lost to Fulford |
| 1992 | Men | Daventry and District<br>S.Rooney 7, D.Gill 5 | Lost to Falkirk |
| 1996 | Men | Northampton<br>G.H.Keates 1,<br>M.J.Izzard 5 | Beat Little Chalfont<br>Lost to Weston-super-<br>Mare (Winners 1996) |

Interestingly, despite the fact that to win the trophy a pair would need to play something in the region of twelve matches, the national trophy was actually retained in 1979 by a pair from Dirleton Castle Lothians.

*Northampton golfers on the first tee at Aloha, Spain 1981.*

# Club Trip to Spain 1981

The Club under the grateful organisation of Derek Holland took a group of some thirty players and some wives to Torremolinos for a week's golf and entertainment. The San Miquel and Sangria certainly flowed that week. It was a most enjoyable trip where everyone got on well and played some winter golf under the warm Spanish sun. "Del Boy" started the entertainment off as soon as we arrived at Malaga airport by going round upon the luggage collection loop. I have yet to see him move as fast as when instructed by the armed policeman. Grev Faulkner developed the habit of coming in to bed at some ridiculous time. He soon got the message to behave from his roommates, however, when he found his bed had been put in the lift. Charles Bryden stated that he would never go in a car ever again with Alan Linney as a result of the race back from Aloha Golf Club to the hotel. A very bumpy landing at Birmingham Airport returned a well-tanned group of happy golfer to UK shores where the stories of the trip are still told with great fondness.

# The First Five Holes "Club"

The first five holes at Harlestone have witnessed some very unusual starts to a round of golf, where four players have joined what is known in bar talk as the "five hole club". In order to be accepted a player must complete the holes in fifteen strokes or less. This is in fact quite a challenge against a par of nineteen. The following players are "members":-

| Player | Score First Hole | Score Second Hole | Score Third Hole | Score Fourth Hole | Score Fifth Hole |
|---|---|---|---|---|---|
| John Evans Kingsthorpe | Par 4 | Birdie 2 | Birdie 4 | Birdie 3 | Birdie 2 |
| Martin Izzard | Birdie 3 | Par 3 | Eagle 3 | Birdie 3 | Par 3 |
| Martin Izzard | Birdie 3 | Birdie 2 | Eagle 3 | Par 4 | Par 3 |
| Andy Limbert | Birdie 3 | Birdie 2 | Birdie 4 | Birdie 3 | Birdie 2 |
| Alex Wray | Eagle 2 | Birdie 2 | Eagle 3 | Bogey 5 | Par 3 |

# Low Front Nine at Harlestone

A record score for the front nine holes of 29 was recorded by Simon Tootell in July 2000 during a friendly fourball. Simon recorded a remarkable sequence of 4 3 4 3 2 3 4 3 3, which included the unique run of birdie, birdie, birdie, eagle, par, birdie, birdie from the third hole to score seven under par for seven holes.

# National Winners.........Very Nearly

Dominic Jessup almost put the Club on to the map at National level in 1999. Playing in the English Open Mid-Amateur Championship at Little Aston, Dominic scored 74,71,73 to finish joint runner up to Yorkshireman

Steven East. He needed a birdie on the final hole to force a play-off for the Logan Trophy but sadly his birdie putt slipped by. Dominic's score of two over for three rounds being an excellent performance on a tough, though delightful course.

The author and partner Glenn Keates finished all square in the National Finals of the Portugolfe competition at Vila Sol on the Algarve. In order to provide a result for the press, we played sudden death after several beers, despite having a gentlemen's agreement the previous night if we did finish all square with our opponents. Glenn to this date maintains that we lost on the nineteenth, I maintain that we finished all square. I will leave the reader to comment on the true final score. A week in Portugal for £22 can't be bad, whatever the result! To date the author and Glenn have notched up an incredible winning tally of 104 wins from 120 matches at Club, County and National level and need a break from this "marriage"!

## Jeremy "Shanky" Shepherd

This blond-haired lover of golf joined the Club in 1988 and rapidly made an impact on the Club golfing and social scene, where he won Club trophies such as Summer Knockout in 1991, the Spencer Cup and Presidents Trophy in 1992 with Millennium Captain Tony Harrison and the Matchplay Championship in 1994. His four iron from the second bunker on the fourth hole on to the green during sudden death is etched in the Club's Hollingsworth history. His nickname of Shanky is obvious to all golfers and often gently described lovingly by his long time Club partner Andy Carter. Sadly in the year 2000, Jeremy suffered a major heart attack (technically an acute dissection of the ascending aorta) at the tender age of thirty-nine. The Club held its breath and gave "thought strength" during Jeremy's three weeks in a coma away from our normal world. We all wish him well, for a strong recovery to his gentlemanly and humorous self.

## Ryder Cup

"I don't think you would have missed that putt but I don't think you should have the opportunity to try". Jack Nicklaus's historic gesture to Tony Jacklin on the 18th green in the 1969 Ryder Cup at Royal Birkdale G.C. which ensured a halved match? A mark of one of the world's best sportsmen, which upset the American Captain in his quest for victory. This sequence of events stands as one of the great sporting gestures of all time.

Can you see such things happening in modern times? For example by Justin Leonard? He had the opportunity at Brookline in 1999, after the famous green invasion, to restore some gentlemanly order. He failed to grasp the opportunity as one who could have changed the nature of the outcome of this dreadful episode of the so-called "Professional" game. If he had conceded Jose Maria Olazabal's putt for a half after the American team had trampled all over the line, the game would have benefited greatly. I was very upset by this whole episode, which typified how the interpersonal standards in life have deteriorated in "certain circles"

*Augusta National. The Masters' Clubhouse and Magnolia Drive looking away from and to Washington Road.*

189

## Masters Sunday and Robert Harris

In April at the start of the golfing season this tournament is always tinged with sadness for some members, since we are unable to share it with young Robert Westley "Inch" Harris. Robert was taken ill on "that Masters evening" in 1993 and died of bacterial meningitis at the tender age of sixteen. Robert was about to become one of the Club's first team players under the watchful and loving eyes of his mother Sue and father Martin. Unknown to many members Martin was present despite the emotional trauma, to support the team at the first tee at Oundle G.C. where Robert would have played in his first game. A minute's silence was observed before the match meal. The Robert Harris Trophy is played for each year by teams consisting of two males, one female and a Junior member of the Club, in memory of this fine young man. Robert had a great sense of humour and many friends at the Club. All monies raised at this event are fittingly donated to the Meningitis Research fund. The ex-Juniors such as Simon Bunn, Ian Jones, Jon Lloyd et al who grew up as golfers with Robert, still talk of him to this day with great affection; he clearly made an impression on them.

## Tiger Woods Phenomena

*"You have enormous responsibility. Remember you have an obligation to protect the integrity of the game of golf. It's all right here, the responsibility is on your shoulders".*

Arnold Palmer, Bay Hill's presentation ceremony, 2000, with his large and friendly hand placed on Tiger Wood's broad shoulders, as if to pass on the responsibility.

*"Remember the date of April the eighth, two thousand and one, when Tiger Woods found his own definition of greatness, for which there is no peer".*

Jim Nantz, CBS TV, when Tiger became the first ever holder of all four major trophies

## St Andrews the Home of Golf

If you have not made the pilgrimage north to the home of golf, "The Auld Gray Toon", I would recommend it strongly to any golfer to realise what are the traditions of the game. The place is absolutely mind-blowing, to walk around the town and down on to the first tee in front of the Royal and Ancient Clubhouse makes you weak at the knees. Golf has been played there since 1400 AD. There are in fact six public courses making Europe's largest golf complex with 99 holes that are managed by the St Andrews Links Trust. The Royal and Ancient Golf Club was founded by 22 noblemen, professors and landowners and played its first medal there in1754. It is the foremost Golf Club in the world, and now governs the rules everywhere together with

*Tiger Woods, the first player to hold all four major trophies, at St. Andrews 2000.*

the U.S.G.A. The current membership is limited to 1800. The Open Championship for the Claret Jug was first played for there in 1873 and was won by Tom Kidd with a score of 179 ahead of the 25 other entrants. Of the six courses the Old Course at 6566 yards par 71 is the most famous and popular. The New Course, at 6604 yards, is over one hundred years old! Golfers are asked to wear "soft spikes" and all fourballs should be completed in 3 hours 45 minutes. Quite how Millennium winner Tiger Woods managed to plot his way round The Old Course for four rounds without going in a bunker to become the Millenium Open Champion and to complete the Grand Slam is astonishing. Some of the bunkers are bordering on the ridiculous, especially the road bunker on seventeenth, though it makes the hole. Since the Old Course is common land one can appreciate what feelings the players have felt over the many years by walking the course when it is quiet, especially the first and eighteenth holes.

*"When the crowds are long gone and the stands dismantled, an eerie stillness lingers as the course rests at the setting of the sun. Shadows of the past creep on to the course and sounds of distant voices heralding triumph or disaster seem to echo around this hallowed ground which is the old course, in ST ANDREWS – THE HOME OF GOLF"*

## Life Overall

"In the long history of humankind (and animal kind, too) those who learned to collaborate and improvise most effectively have prevailed."

CHARLES DARWIN, THE ORIGIN OF SPECIES 1859.

**THE OVERTONES FROM THIS QUOTATION COULD BE SYMPATHETICALLY HEAPED UPON THE GREATEST GAME MAN HAS EVER PLAYED OVER SIX CENTURIES, OUR GAME OF GOLF WHICH CONTINUES TO PROMOTE THE TRUE VALUES OF LIFE WHICH ARE TIMELESS.**

**Martin John Izzard**

**March 2002**

*The old and new clubhouses at Kettering Road and Harlestone.*

# REFERENCES

1. G.Sibley Northampton Golf Club "A Centenary history 1893-1993" 1993 ISBN 0 9520291 0 3 Woolnough Bookbindings Ltd Irthlingborough Northamptonshire.

2. The Northamptonshire Golf Union Yearbooks Ed B.Barron, D.Croxton and M.J.Izzard *et al* 1996-2002.

# SUBSCRIBERS

| Name | Title | Name | Title |
|------|-------|------|-------|
| G.P.Addington | Team Captain 1996-2001 | A.J.Lack | Hollingsworth Team Player 1980's |
| G.Alsop | Member 2002 | A.Lane | Tartan Trophy 1989 *et al* |
| G.R.Ashton | Rabbits Cup 1979 | R.Lane | Member 2002 |
| R.Baker | Frank Wild Cup 1999 | A.J.Limbert | Club Champion 1998 *et al* |
| I.Bailey | Social Member 2002 | J.M.Lloyd | Club Champion 1997 *et al* |
| L.S.Bailey | Member 2002 | J.W.Lloyd | Boys Nett Trophy 1991 |
| S.J.Bailey | Presidents Trophy 1991 *et al* | T.J.Lloyd | Club Captain 1994 |
| E.Barber | Member 2002 | A.J.Linney | Club Champion 1983 *et al* |
| A.J.Basham | Robert Harris fun-day 2000 | R.Mabbutt | Member 2002 |
| A.R.Bason | Spencer Cup 1998 | C.MacKenzie | County Handicap Challenge Cup 1992 *et al* |
| R.W.Bason | Dawland Cup 1990 | P.F.McKenzie | Dazeley Trophy 1986 *et al* |
| P.Beeby | The Golfer 1975 *et al* | P.D.Miller | Member & Advertiser |
| J.D.Bird | Grandfather Putter 1994 | A.R.Moir | The Golfer 1976 *et al* |
| M.J.Blake | Soutar Cup 1995 | J.J.Moorcroft | County Stableford Cup Winner 1989 |
| D.G.Blundell | Member 2002 | | |
| K.E.Bonham | Frank Wild Cup 1984 | T.Murfin | Presidents Trophy 1982 |
| T.P.Bott | Member 2002 | S.Newman | Member 2002 |
| A.Bowen | Frank Wild 1980 | Northamptonshire Golf Union | |
| G.W.Bradbury | Member 2002 | P.Ollive | Dazeley Trophies 1993 *et al* |
| C.Bridgewater | Veterans Cup 1993 | B.Page | Coronation Cup 1987 *et al* |
| K.Brownless | Northampton Cup 1987 *et al* | R.Page | Stanhope Cup 1981 *et al* |
| S.J.Bunn | Nett League Championship 1996 | A.J.Peacock | County Stableford Cup 1997 *et al* |
| F.Bustin | Millenium Trophy 2000 *et al* | C.G.Peacock | Club Captain 1999 |
| J.Campbell-Jones | County Stableford Cup 1998 | J.Pennington | Dawland Cup 2001 |
| L.J.Cantrell | County Captain 1996-2000 | M.W.Pepper | Junior Organizer 1999-2000 |
| A.J.Carter | Club Champion 1989 *et al* | M.J.Pound | Presidents Trophy 2000 *et al* |
| D.J.Carter | Member 2002 | D.C.Prior | Club Captain 1990 |
| J.A.Churchman | Tartan Trophy 2002 | J.R.F.Pulford | Member & Advertiser |
| K.J.Coles | Presidents Trophy 1995 *et al* | G.J.Riddall | Club Match Play Champion 1990 *et al* |
| G.Condon | The Golfer 1997 *et al* | D.J.Roberts | Presidents Trophy 2001 |
| J.Craddock | Vaughan Morris 1992 et al | I.P.Robins | Silver Salvers 1987 *et al* |
| W.Craghill | Member 2002 & Advertiser | B.Russell | Soutar Cup 1976 *et al* |
| D&P.Dare | Trahearn Trophy 1997 *et al* | J.Shepherd | Club Match Play Champion 1994 *et al* |
| V.Davies | Member 2002 | G.H.Slinn | Northampton Cup 1995 *et al* |
| T.Doran | Advertiser | E.Smith | Member 2002 |
| S.J.Eborall | Presidents Trophy 1994 *et al* | M.S.Smith | Club Captain 1998 |
| A.J.Field | County Senior Nett Champion 1998 | R.G.Soloman | Frank Wild 1986 *et al* |

G.Fitzwilliams Rabbits Cup 1991

T.B.Flynn Dawland Cup 1976

J.S.Forbear Member and Supporter

B.J.Frost Club Captain 1988

N.J.Frost Dawland Cup 1991 *et al*

R.A.Frost Club Captain 1996

G.Garbutt Club Captain 1993

R.W.Glass Wellingborough Cup 1989

J.A.Graham Frank Wild 1987

I.J.Griffiths Dawland Cup1993

J.Halliwell Club Captain 1977

P.Halliwell Member 2002

J.Hallwood Wellingborough Cup 1987 *et al*

P.Hallwood Dazeley Trophy 1991 *et al*

G.S.Hammon Member and Advertiser

G.E.Hanson Presidents Trophy 1989

K.Hanwell Midland Ladies Champion 2001 *et al*

M&S.Harris Donors of Robert Harris Cup *et al*

R.J.Hawkins Member 2002

K.Heard Presidents Trophy 1994 *et al*

M.Heath Trahearn trophy 1995&9 *et al*

R.Heath Lady Captain 2001

D.G.Hoblin Captain's Weekend (Sat) 1993

D.J.Holland President's Trophy 1983 *et al*

A.M.Hughes Rabbits Cup 1997

P.R.Huntley Club Captain 1996

L.Inwood Lady Captain 2002

A.J.Izzard County Boys Champion 2000 *et al*

D.J.Jessup Club Champion 1993 *et al*

I.Jones Junior Captain 1994

C.Johnson The Golfer 1994 *et al*

G.Keates Club Captain 2001

G.H.Keates County Champion 1998 *et al*

F.A.B.King Member 2002

G.Knight Junior Captain 2000

T.C.A.Knight Club President

N.Soto County Champion 1999 & 2001

B.J.Stanbridge Silver Salvers 1989 *et al*

A.Stensones Spencer Cup 1993

A.F.Stevens County President 1990-92

G.S.Stewart Soutar Cup 2000 *et al*

F.M.Storr Vaughan Morris 1985

P.S.Taylor Wellingborough Cup 1999 *et al*

M.C.Thatcher Soutar Cup 1983

S.Thornhill Member 2002

S.Trout Junior Organiser 1994-7

C.J.Turner Northampton Cup 1968 *et al*

D.E.Tyrell Lady Captain 1982

D.N.Tyrell Semi Finalist, Presidents Trophy 1983

M.E.Underwood Member 2002

G.H.Upwood Chairman M.G.U.

K.J.Vallance Presidents Trophy 1968 & 1988 *et al*

R.T.F.Willoughby Northampton Cup 1989, Presidents 1993

J.A.Wilmer Club Captain 2002

P.Worrall Member 2002

# INDEX

**Bold Text** = Picture, Normal Text = Page Number.

**Units 6-8**
**Wheatfield Road South**
**Abington**
**Northampton**
**NN3 2HH**

*Director: A.J. Carter*

**Telephone (01604) 408999**
**Fax (01604) 415498**
**Mobile 07885 744414**

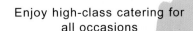